EASY TO COOK BOOK

Carolyn Zervudachi

EASY
TO
COOK
BOOK

ANDRE DEUTSCH

First published 1984 by
André Deutsch Limited
105 Great Russell Street
London WC1

Black and white drawings by Chen Ling.
Colour photographs by Mike Leale.
Phototypeset by Falcon Graphic Art Ltd,
Wallington, Surrey
Printed in Great Britain by
R.J. Acford Ltd, Chichester, Sussex

ISBN 0 233 97698 1

To Nolly

I want to thank Jonathan Raban for all his encouragement and enthusiasm, which got me going; my children, Laky, Paddy, Tino and Manuela and my sister Geraldine Barry for their appreciation and support which kept me going; Cynthia Kee and Stanley Olson for their special help and understanding, and the many other friends and relations who have cooked and eaten their way through this book.

Contents

Before starting these recipes, please read the introductory notes.

Introduction

This book is aimed at all those people who imagine they could never possibly cook, let alone find it easy and enjoyable.

It all started when a friend complained he could no longer afford to entertain his lady friends in restaurants.

'Why not a cosy, intimate dinner at home, in candlelight and privacy?' I suggested.

'I can't cook,' he admitted ruefully.

'I'll write you out one of my recipe charts,' said I brightly. 'Anyone can follow them, or so my family tell me. How about cooking her a soufflé?'

He looked horrified, then disappointed. 'You're joking,' he said.

'I'm not. With my charts, if you can read, you can cook.'

The next evening he telephoned, sounding desperate. 'I'm trying your soufflé chart, but what on earth – I mean – I know how to fold a shirt, or a deckchair – but how do you fold whites of eggs?' Clearly, some explanatory notes were essential.

A few days later he telephoned again. 'I must have more charts!'

More charts were duly produced, and to my delight these were seized on not only by my friend, but by my teenage children as well. 'It's really fun,' they exclaimed. 'Like a treasure hunt.'

The charts themselves are self-explanatory. Following the step-by-step instructions from left to right, you can't go wrong, even with things that are supposed to be unpredictable, like soufflés. The middle column – the ingredients – is shaded, so that you know at a glance what your shopping list should be. **The recipes are all for two people,** since I find multiplying easier than dividing.

I have tried to give a good balance of about a hundred recipes from which anyone can put a meal together. Essential ingredients and utensils, together with hints about easy measuring methods, cooking temperatures, etc., are given in the opening pages. For the charts to work, you *must* read these pages – for example, a teaspoon or tablespoon of flour or sugar is always a level spoonful.

Remember, anyone can cook. It is simply a question of having the information about what to do with what, when and how. The charts give you this. Follow them, and discover all the delights of home cooking!

Weighing and Measuring

In the following recipes, I have given weights in ounces and grams, e.g. 2oz/56g. If you have kitchen scales, well and good. If not, it is usually possible to make a reasonable estimate (2oz butter will be a quarter of your half-pound pat).

It is essential, however, that the weights of certain dry ingredients are accurate, and these I have given in teaspoons and tablespoons. These spoons are always level. Simply scoop up the flour, sugar or whatever with the spoon, and level it off with a knife or a finger.

Always remember when using this book:
1 teasp   = 1 level teaspoonful
1 tabls   = 1 level tablespoonful

Here are some easy guides to dry weights:

For flour, cornflour, cocoa:
2 teasp   = ¼oz = 7g
4 teasp   = ½oz = 14g
1 tabls   = ½oz = 14g
2 tabls   = 1oz = 28g
4 standard teacups = 1lb = 450g

For sugar, rice, lentils, etc.:
1 tabls   = 1oz = 28g
3 standard teacups = 1lb
                   = 450g

For breadcrumbs:
1 tabls   = ¼oz = 7g

Liquid measurements are given in pints and millilitres, e.g. ½pt/280ml. A half-pint measuring jug is the best thing for measuring liquids, but failing that you can always keep a ¼pint and a ½pint plastic yoghourt or cream container on hand.

Where liquid quantities are very small, I have given them in teaspoons and tablespoons – there should be no difficulty in making sure these are level!

Handy rough measurements are:
8 tabls = ¼pt = 1 standard teacup = approx 140 ml
1 standard coffee mug or tumbler = approx ½pt = approx 280ml
1pt = 560 ml

Cooking Temperatures

In order to simplify these charts, I use only four heats: very low, low, medium and hot. These are equivalent to the following oven temperatures:

Very Low   = 250°F   = 110°C   = gas mark ½
Low   = 300°F   = 140°C   = gas mark 2
Medium   = 350°F   = 180°C   = gas mark 4-5
Hot   = 400°F   = 190°C   = gas mark 7

Cooking Times

I have given an overall time for each recipe. These are all approximations, to give you some idea of how long each dish will take to prepare and cook. Some people work faster than others.

Sugar

Where a recipe requires brown, or caster, sugar, I have specified this. Where I say simply 'sugar', use ordinary white granulated sugar.

Parsley

I think very many dishes look and taste better when garnished with parsley, and this is the last instruction on many of the charts. It is, however, not essential.

Utensils

I. THE BARE ESSENTIALS

Pans
    1 small milk pan
    1 medium saucepan with lid
    1 large saucepan with lid
    1 frying pan
Knives
    1 long, sharp knife for meat, etc.
    1 short, serrated knife for vegetables, etc.
Half-pint measuring jug

Standard-size tablespoon for measuring (18ml)
Standard-size teaspoon for measuring (5ml)

Sieve-strainer
2 wooden spoons
Rotary egg-beater
Tin-opener
Potato masher
Four-sided grater with different gauges on each side
2 mixing bowls
Ovenproof casserole with lid

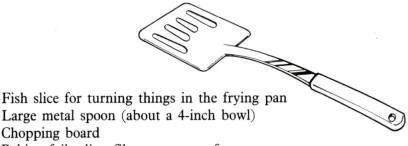

Fish slice for turning things in the frying pan
Large metal spoon (about a 4-inch bowl)
Chopping board
Baking foil, cling film, greaseproof paper
Lemon/orange squeezer

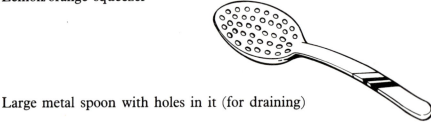

Large metal spoon with holes in it (for draining)

II. BAKING AND SOUFFLES

2 cake tins the same size, about 7 inches in diameter
Baking tray
Wire cake cooling rack
Flan tin or dish (about 7 inches in diameter)
3 ovenproof dishes, small, medium and large
Ring mould (about 9 inches)
Soufflé dish   6 inches (15cm) in diameter for two people, 8 inches (25cm)
    in diameter for six. Soufflés may be made in any ovenproof dish, but
    the proper, correct-sized dish makes perfect results more likely.

III. USEFUL EXTRAS

Kitchen scissors
Colander

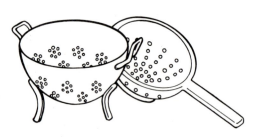

Electric kettle
Soup ladle
Good set of kitchen knives with knife-sharpener
Large spaghetti saucepan
Serrated bread knife

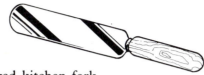

Palette knife
Long-handled 2- or 3-pronged kitchen fork
Screw-top jar for storing vinaigrette
Liquidizer: well worth investing in. I think a Kenwood Mixer with attachments is best, but if this is beyond your means, an electric liquidizer on its own is much cheaper. So is an electric rotary beater on its own. Failing any of these, a hand-operated Mouli mill is an effective liquidizer – or you can do it the long, hard way with a sieve.

Ingredients

I. YOUR BASIC LARDER

Salt
Pepper
Mustard
Eggs
Milk
Flour: plain and self-raising
Butter or Margarine
Sugar
Cooking oil
Vinegar
Cooking cheese (of your choice)
Lemon juice (fresh or bottled)
Tinned tomatoes
Rice
Spaghetti
Cornflour
Chicken stock cubes
Tomato puree

Spices: nutmeg, cinnamon, ginger, curry powder, paprika
Dried herbs: mixed herbs are essential, separate packets of basil, marjoram, tarragon and bay leaves highly desirable.
Garlic: powder or chopped garlic for emergencies. Fresh garlic lasts quite a while.
Vanilla

II. VEGETABLES TO BUY IN REGULARLY

Potatoes
Onions
Carrots
Celery
Parsley

III. HELPFUL INSTANT AIDS

Frozen vegetables: especially peas and spinach
Frozen pastry: especially puff pastry. Shortcrust pastry is easier to make.
Mayonnaise: Hellmans, or a supermarket's own-brand real mayonnaise
Bisto gravy thickener (for thickening and colour; has practically no flavour)
Easy-to-cook rice: e.g. Uncle Ben's
Arrowroot: the best emergency thickener

Hints for Beginners

I. EGGS

Boiling

Two ways to make the perfectly boiled egg.

A. 1. Bring a small saucepan of water to the boil.
   2 Add a dash of vinegar. (This helps to prevent the egg from coming out of the shell if the shell cracks.)
   3. Prick one end of the egg with a pin (this helps to prevent the shell from cracking) and put the egg in the boiling water.
   4. When the water is boiling again, turn the heat down to medium and simmer for exactly four minutes.

B. 1. Put a pierced egg in a small saucepan and cover it with cold water and a dash of vinegar.
   2. Bring the water to the boil.
   3. When it is boiling, let it bubble for exactly one minute.

Separating yolks from whites

You usually do this in order to whip the whites. The whites will not whip satisfactorily if the beater or bowl is wet, so always use dry utensils.

Conventional method:
   1. Crack the egg carefully, gently but firmly, on the edge of a mixing bowl.

2. Hold one half of the egg in one hand between fingers and thumb, the other half in the same way in the other hand, and prise the two halves apart carefully, letting the white slip out and into the bowl beneath.

3. Transfer the yolk carefully from one half of the shell to the other and back again, gradually letting the white drop into the bowl, until you have separated as much of the white as possible from the yolk. Put the yolk into another bowl.

Your white is now ready for whipping, and your yolk for whatever your recipe tells you to do with it.

If, in spite of your concentration, you break the yolk so that the white cannot be separated, use that egg for something else and start again; if there is yolk in with the white, it will not whip properly.

Easy method:
1. Break the egg carefully into a saucer.
2. Put an egg-cup upside down over the yolk.

3. Hold the egg-cup firmly in place and tip the saucer over a bowl so that the white slides off the saucer and down into the bowl. This way, you don't get yolk in the white nearly so often. A tiny drop can always be fished out with a teaspoon.

Whipping egg whites   You can use either a hand- or electrically-operated rotary beater, or even a wire whisk or a fork – but these last two take ages to do the job. Add a pinch of salt to the whites, and whip them firmly until they are white and fluffy, and stiff enough to stand up in points.

Folding in egg whites   This is necessary, for example, when making a soufflé. The idea of folding is to allow as much air as possible to stay in the mixture you are folding.

1. You have the yolk mixture in a pan or bowl, and the stiffly whipped whites in a bowl.
2. Pour the mixture into the bowl of egg whites.

3. Take a large metal spoon, hold it at the angle shown in the sketch, and turn the bowl as you are mixing.
4. On the down-stroke, take the egg white down in the bowl of the spoon, and turn the spoon at the bottom of the bowl so that you bring the mixture up and over the egg white.
5. Continue to mix, as quickly and lightly as possible, using the folding motion described, always taking the spoon from the top to the bottom, back to the top and over, until the mixture is evenly distributed, and the consistency is light and frothy.

Tips for successful soufflés

1. A soufflé always looks better in the right size of dish (see page xii). Remember that the uncooked mixture should be within half an inch of the top of the dish.
2. Open the oven door as little as possible while the soufflé is cooking, and serve it immediately it is cooked. Soufflés sink easily and fast.

II. RICE AND PASTA

Rice and pasta are delicious, when cooked properly, and extremely useful as last-minute resorts if you suddenly want to produce a substantial meal for any number. Often they come in packets with instructions – in which case, obviously, you simply follow them. If there are no instructions, this is what you do:

1. Bring to the boil a large saucepan of water.
2. Add 3 teaspoons of salt.
3. Add the rice or pasta.
4. Stir immediately with a large spoon or fork for one or two minutes, until the water is boiling again.
5. Turn the heat down to Low, so that the water is simmering (i.e. boiling gently).
6. If it is rice you are cooking, cover the saucepan; if it is pasta, do not cover the saucepan, as it will boil over. In either case, let the water simmer for ten to fifteen minues. Stir occasionally and test the rice or pasta after ten minutes. Some brands cook more quickly than others, and you can only tell as you go along. For example, most brown rice takes much longer to cook than white rice, and fresh pasta needs only a few minutes' boiling time.
7. When the consistency is to your liking, pour the contents of the saucepan through a strainer and quickly run cold water over the rice or pasta for a few seconds. Shake the strainer to get most – but not all – of the water out. If it gets too dry it will stick together. If it *does* stick together, run some more cold water over it.

8. Tip it quickly back into the saucepan, add a lump of butter and/or some olive oil, whichever you prefer, grind black pepper over it and cover the saucepan until you are ready to serve. Pasta should be served as soon as possible, but rice can be kept warm for a while in a dish in a warm oven.

9. If something goes wrong, and when you come to serve the rice or pasta you find it all stuck together, add a cup of hot water little by little and stir with a fork.

III. ONIONS

Chopping

1. Use your sharpest vegetable knife.
2. Cut off the top and the root, and remove the skin under cold running water.

3. Cut the onion in half from the top end to the root end so

4. Place the two halves flat sides down on the chopping board so

5. Slice the halves crossways, holding what become the crescent-shaped slices together, as you slice as evenly as you can.
6. Turn the sliced half-onion 90° holding the slices together, and slice crossways again.

How to Avoid Tears

The only sure way to avoid tears when chopping onions is to use a machine – either a food processor or a hand-operated chopper. Different cooks have different solutions to offer, however. Here are a few:

1. Avoid breathing in the smell by holding your head well back as you chop.

2. Put the onion skin on your head while you are chopping!
3. If you have a gas cooker, chop the onion next to the lighted flame of the gas ring. I do this, and switch on the extractor fan over my cooker, so I never cry.

IV. POTATOES

Boiling New Potatoes
1. Scrub them well: a pan-scourer (not the soapy kind) is ideal for this.
2. Put them in a saucepan and cover them with cold water.
3. Add 1 teaspoon salt.
4. Bring them to the boil, then turn down the heat and let them boil gently for about ½-¾ hour.
5. Drain off the water and toss the potatoes in butter and chopped mint.

Boiling Old Potatoes
1. Peel them, and cut into pieces of about 1½inches/40cm square.
2. Put them in a saucepan and cover them with cold water.
3. Add 1 teaspoon salt.
4. Bring them to the boil.
5. Cover pan, and cook steadily on a medium heat for ½-¾ hour.
6. Drain off the water and toss the potatoes in butter, chopped parsley, salt and pepper.

Baking Potatoes in their Jackets

A. Whole
   1. Scrub them well.
   2. Rub them with oil.
   3. Put them on the rack in a hot oven for about 1 hour, or until tender.
   4. To serve, make a cross incision on their tops, and insert a generous lump of butter and a sprig of parsley.

B. Halved
   1. Scrub them well.
   2. Rub them with oil.
   3. Cut them in half lengthways.
   4. Sprinkle white flesh side with salt.
   5. Put them on the rack in a hot oven white side up for about ½-1 hour till the tops are brown and the flesh is tender.

Mashing
1. Peel and slice the potatoes.
2. Put them in a saucepan and cover them with water.
3. Add 1 teaspoon salt.
4. Bring to the boil.
5. Lower the heat and cook steadily for about ½ hour until tender.
6. Drain off the water and mash the potatoes with a potato masher – a fork will do at a pinch.
7. Add milk, butter, pepper and salt to taste.
8. Beat well with a wooden spoon.

To Sauté

1. Peel the potatoes and cut them into bite-size pieces, or slice them.
2. Melt 1 tablespoon butter and 1 tablespoon oil together in a frying pan.
3. Add the potatoes and stir and fry them until they are brown and tender.

Roasting

1. Peel the potatoes and cut them into pieces of about 1½in/40cm square.
2. Put them in a saucepan and cover them with water.
3. Add 1 teaspoon salt.
4. Bring to the boil, and allow to boil steadily for 3 minutes.
5. Drain off the water.
6. Run cold water over the potatoes for ½ minute.
7. Put them round the roasting meat in the oven

   or

   in a separate roasting tin containing two tablespoons of pre-heated oil.
8. Cook for 1 hour, turning two or three times.

V. LEFTOVERS

Reheating things which have been cooked in water
(e.g. rice, plain boiled vegetables, etc.)

1. Bring to the boil 4 tablespoons water.
2. Add a knob of butter and melt it.
3. Add the rice, or whatever, and heat it through over a very low heat, stirring carefully with a wooden spoon.
4. It should be evenly heated through in a few minutes.

Reheating things which have been cooked in milk or cream
(e.g. mashed potatoes, anything in white sauce, etc.)

1. Bring to the boil 4 tablespoons milk.
2. Add a knob of butter and melt it.
3. Add the mashed potatoes, or whatever, and heat through over a very low heat, stirring *very* carefully with a wooden spoon (things cooked with milk or cream tend to be more delicate).
4. It should be evenly heated through in a few minutes.

Four tablespoons water or milk is enough to reheat servings for two people; use more for larger quantities, and add more if the dish seems too dry.

Reheating oven-cooked dishes
These can simply be popped back in the oven, pre-heated to Hot. Ten to fifteen minutes should be long enough, but test the middle of the dish to check that it is heated through before serving. Even soufflés can be reheated in this way.

VI. HANDY TIPS

Wash up as you go along

This is particularly sensible if you do not have a vast array of utensils, and if your cooking area is a small one, which is very often the case. Use one bowl and spoon then wash them, instead of reaching for clean ones. Your labours in the kitchen will seem less, and you will not be faced with a discouraging mountain of washing-up after your meal.

Especially when handling onions, garlic or fish
The smell and taste of these three linger on hands, knives, pans, etc. Wash anything that has been in contact with them in cold water before using it for anything else. For example, if you use a knife which has just chopped garlic to cut the butter for your chocolate mousse, the latter may well be ruined by the distinctive flavour of the former!

Thinning sauces

If a sauce is too thick, add milk or water little by little until it has the right consistency, letting the sauce cook gently over a medium heat and stirring all the time.

Thickening sauces

If a sauce is too thin:
1. Mix 1 teaspoonful cornflour and 4 tablespoons cold milk or water in a small bowl.
2. Stir this until it is smooth.
3. Take the pan off the heat and add the cornflour mixture, stirring well.
4. Return the pan to the heat and bring the sauce to the boil, stirring all the time.
5. Let it cook for a minute or two over a medium heat, stirring constantly, until it is thick and smooth.

If you have arrowroot, sprinkle a teaspoonful over the too-thin sauce, stir well, and allow it to cook for a minute or two.

Boiling vegetables

Fresh, plain boiled vegetables are delicious, as long as they are not overcooked. Don't use too much water (only potatoes need to be covered), and keep testing with a knife or fork after ten minutes. When the knife or fork goes right through a sprout or cauliflower stem, the vegetables are ready, and should be drained immediately. If they are cooked any longer they will be soggy, and lose their flavour.

Seasoning

The amounts of salt and pepper you use are a matter of personal taste, so I haven't been specific. A good general rule, however, when adding salt to liquid, is to add at least a half teaspoonful per pint.

Stirring

Always remember to use a *wooden* spoon, except where the recipe specifies a metal one.

1. Aubergines stuffed with Tomato and Mozzarella
See recipe 25

2. Lamb Chops with Lemon and Orange Sauce and Garlic *See recipe 57*

1 Carrot, Onion and Orange Soup

**Overall time:
30 mins**

This soup is equally good hot or cold. If you are making a cold soup, cook it early on, to give it time to get really cold in the refrigerator before serving.

Process	Amount	Ingredients	Explanation	Time	Heat
1. Peel and chop	1 medium	Onion			
2. Scrape and chop	2 large	Carrots			
3. Melt in a saucepan	1oz/28g	Butter	Add the onions and carrots. Stir and cook	5 min	Med
4. Add and stir well	¾pt/420ml	Water			
5. Add and dissolve	1	Chicken cube	Bring to the boil	3 min	Hot
6. Season with		Salt, Pepper	Stir in. Cover pan. Cook	20 min	Med
7. Add and stir well	8 tabls	Orange Juice	Put through a sieve, or liquidize		
8. If serving hot. . . Reheat soup. Chop fine	2 teasp	Parsley	Sprinkle parsley over each plate of soup		
Alternatively If serving cold Chill soup. Chop fine	2 teasp	Chives	Sprinkle chives over each plate of soup		

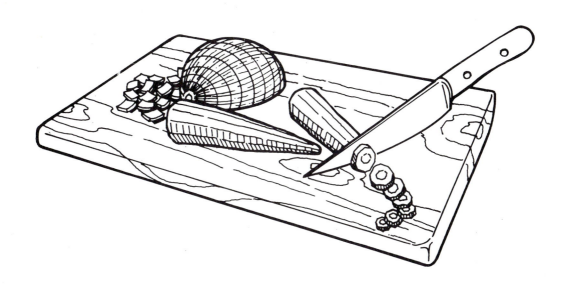

Cheese and Onion Soup

A variation on the traditional French onion soup. Simple and satisfying.

Overall time:
30 mins

Process	Amount	Ingredients	Explanation	Time	Heat
1. Peel and chop	1 medium	Onion	In little pieces		
2. Melt	1oz/28g	Butter	In a saucepan	1 min	Hot
3. Add chopped onions			Cook, stirring constantly	8 min	Med
4. Add and stir well	1 tabls	Plain Flour			
5. Add and stir well	1pt/560ml	Water	Bring to the boil, stir	2 min	Hot
6. Add and stir well	½	Chicken cube	Until dissolved		
7. Season with		Salt, Pepper	Cover pan and cook	15 min	Low
8. Liquidize or mash			With a potato masher		
9. Grate and stir well	3oz/84g	Cheese	Into the onion soup		V.Low
10. Heat and stir			Till cheese melts (do *not* allow to boil) for	3 min	Low
11. Chop	1 teasp	Parsley	Sprinkle parsley over each plate of soup.		

3   Clam Chowder

Overall time:
1 hr

A wonderfully satisfying soup, especially on a cold winter's night. You can make it even more fortifying by adding other vegetables at the start, such as carrots, turnips, beans, peppers, etc.

Process	Amount	Ingredients	Explanation	Time	Heat
1. Peel and chop finely	1 medium	Onion			
2. Melt in a saucepan	1oz/28g	Butter			
3. De-rind and add	2 slices	Bacon	Cook till brown	2 min	Hot
4. Remove bacon from pan			Add onions. Cook and stir	3 min	Med
			Cut bacon in small bits and put back in the pan		Low
5. De-string and chop	1 big stick	Celery	Add to onions and bacon		Low
6. Peel, chop and add	1 medium	Potato	Stir well together	1 min	Hot
7. Add and stir well	1pt/560ml	Water	Bring to the boil		Hot
8. Season with	1 teasp 1	Salt, Pepper, Paprika Bayleaf	Stir well together. Lower heat. Cover pan. Cook	25 min	Low
9. Remove from heat			Mash coarsely with a potato masher		
10. Add	5 tabls	Tinned Corn	Stir well in		
11. Add	5 tabls	Tinned Clams	Mix well together and bring to the boil	2min	Hot
12. Lower heat. Chop fine	4 teasp	Parsley	Add half the parsley to soup and cook gently	1 min	Low
13. Add and stir well	6 tabls	Milk/Cream	Reheat gently (do *not* boil)	1 min	Med
14. Serve the soup			Sprinkled with the rest of the parsley		

4 Artichoke Soup

A lovely soup even without the shellfish, but adding the clams and especially oysters is a delicious luxury surprise.

Overall time:
1 hr

Process	Amount	Ingredients	Explanation	Time	Heat
1. Peel and chop	1lb/450g	Jerusalem Artichokes	Put in cold water		
2. Peel and chop	1 medium	Onion			
3. Melt in a saucepan	1oz/28g	Butter	Add onions. Cook and stir	3 min	Med
4. Drain the artichokes			Add them to the onions. Cook, stirring occasionally	10 min	Low
5. Stir in	¾pt/420ml	Water			
6. Add and dissolve	½	Chicken cube	Bring to the boil	2 min	Hot
7. Season with		Salt, Pepper	Cover pan. Cook gently	20 min	Low
8. Sieve or liquidize the mixture			Return it to the pan		
9. Add and stir well in	¼pt/140ml	Milk	Cook and stir till hot	2-3 min	Hot
10. Chop finely	2 teasp	Parsley	Sprinkle over each plate of soup		
Optional: Add	2 or 2oz/56g	Oysters or Clams (fresh or tinned)	To the soup at the same time as the milk		

5   Leek Soup with Bacon

Overall time:
30 mins

The flavour and the crispness of bacon goes especially well with leeks. It is excellent without liquidizing, if you like a rougher texture.

Process	Amount	Ingredients	Explanation	Time	Heat
1. Wash very carefully	3 medium	Leeks	Cut in quarters and slice very fine		
2. Melt	1oz/28g	Butter	In a saucepan	1 min	Hot
3. Add the leeks. Stir			With a wooden spoon	5 min	Med
4. Add and stir well	¾pt/420ml	Water	Bring to the boil	2 min	Hot
5. Add and stir well	1	Chicken cube	Until dissolved		
6. Season with		Salt, Pepper	Cover pan and cook	15 min	Low
7. De-rind and cut	2 slices	Bacon	In tiny bits		
8. Heat in a frying pan	2 teasp	Oil	Add bacon. Fry till crisp Remove and keep warm	1½ min	Hot
9. Liquidize or mouli the leeks and liquid			Return to saucepan		
10. Add and stir	6 tabls	Milk/Cream	Reheat but *do not* boil	1 min	Hot
11. Serve			Sprinkled with the bacon bits		

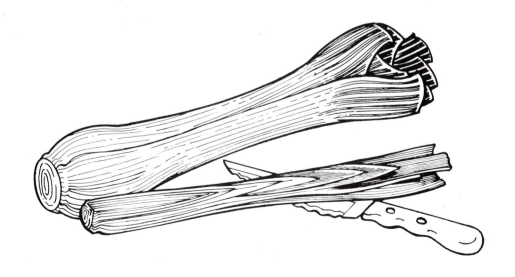

6 Hot Cucumber Soup

Overall time: 25 min

An unusual way to have cucumber soup. See if your guest can guess what it's made of . . . difficult, even when it's served cold, because cooking the cucumber makes that subtle difference.

Process	Amount	Ingredients	Explanation	Time	Heat
1. Peel and slice	6"/15cm	Cucumber			
2. Melt	1oz/28g	Butter	In a saucepan	½ min	Hot
3. Add the cucumber			Stir well. Cover pan. Cook	7 min	Low
4. Add and stir well	½pt/280ml	Water	Bring to the boil	2 min	Hot
5. Add and dissolve	½	Chicken cube	Cover pan and cook for	10 min	Low
6. Season with		Salt, Pepper	Sieve or liquidize or mash with potato masher		
7. Add and stir well	8 tabls	Milk/Cream	Heat, stirring constantly	2 min	Hot
8. If serving hot: Chop	2 teasp	Parsley	Sprinkle over each plate of soup		
Alternatively If serving cold: Chill soup. Chop	2 teasp	Mint	Sprinkle mint over each plate of soup		

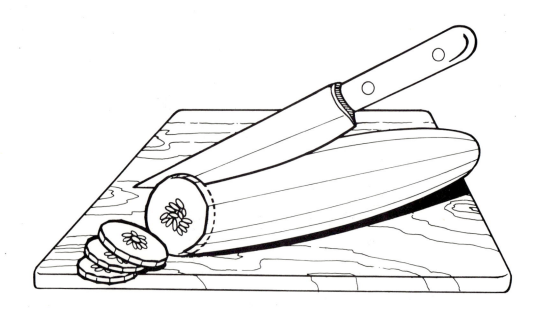

Greek Lentil Soup

A heart-warming soup to satisfy the hungriest appetite. It can be practically a meal in itself.

**Overall time:
2 hrs**

Process	Amount	Ingredients	Explanation	Time	Heat
1. Peel and chop	1 medium	Onion	Very finely		
2. Peel and chop	1 medium	Carrot	Very finely		
3. Put in a saucepan	1½pts/840ml	Water	Add onions and carrots		
4. Clean and rinse well	8oz/225g	Green Lentils	Add to the saucepan. Bring to the boil	5 min	Hot
5. Chop small and add	8oz/225g	Tomatoes (1 small tin)	Stir well together		
6. Season with		Salt, Pepper	Bring to boil again	3 min	Hot
7. Add and stir well	1	Chicken cube			
8. Add and stir in	1 tabls	Olive Oil			
9. Add and stir in	½ teasp	Garlic (powder or fresh)	Cover pan, and cook	1½ hr	Low
10. Check seasoning. Add	1 tabls	Vinegar			
11. Chop finely	2 teasp	Parsley	Sprinkle over each plate.		

Eggs in Artichoke Hearts with Butter Sauce

Such a pretty dish! And it tastes as good as it looks. Preparing the artichokes (steps 13 and 14) takes time.

Overall time:
1¼ hrs

Process	Amount	Ingredients	Explanation	Time	Heat
1. Fill a saucepan with		Water	Bring it to the boil		Hot
2. Add and stir in Add	2 tabls 2 teasp	Vinegar Salt			
3. Cut the stems off	2	Globe Artichokes	Add to water. Cook	30 min	Med
4. Fill a small pan with		Water	Bring to the boil		Hot
5. Put in	2	Eggs	Boil them for *exactly*	6 min	Hot
6. Remove eggs from pan			Put at once in cold water until cool		
7. Crack shells gently			All over with a knife		
8. Remove the shells very carefully			Under a cold running tap		
9. Melt in a small pan	3oz/84g	Butter			
10. Add and stir well in	3 teasp	Plain Flour	Remove pan from heat		
11. Add and stir well in	¼pt/140ml	Milk	Beat with an eggbeater	2 min	Med
12. Season with Add and stir	1 teasp	Salt, Pepper Vinegar	Cook, stirring constantly Cover pan. Lower heat	1 min	Low V.Low
13. Remove the leaves			From the inside of the artichokes, leaving about 12 round the outside		
14. Remove hairy centres with a spoon			Trim leaves to points with scissors		
15. Put the eggs			Into the artichokes		
16. Pour the sauce over the eggs			Serve		

Eggs and Asparagus in White Sauce Gratinée

Overall time: 30 min

An easy and very tasty first course or light lunch dish. You can serve it in an ovenproof dish or in individual cocotte dishes. You can use fresh or frozen asparagus instead of tinned, and parmesan is best but any cheese will do.

Process	Amount	Ingredients	Explanation	Time	Heat
1. Boil in a saucepan	3	Eggs	Covered with water	10 min	Hot
2. Put eggs in			Cold water till cool enough to shell		
3. Meanwhile, melt	2oz/56g	Butter	In a saucepan	1 min	Hot
4. Add and stir well in	3 teasp	Plain Flour	Remove from heat		
5. Add and stir well in	¼pt/140ml	Milk	Return to heat. Boil and beat with an eggbeater	2 min	Med
6. Season with		Salt, Pepper	Stir well. Lower heat		V.Low
7. Drain and stir in gently	1 small tin	Asparagus Tips	Cover pan		V.Low
8. Crack eggshells Peel off the shells			All over with a knife Under the running tap		
9. Cut the eggs in half			Lay in an ovenproof dish or in cocotte dishes		
10. Pour the sauce			Over the eggs		
11. Grate finely	2oz/56g	Cheese	Sprinkle over the sauce		
12. Put under the grill or in the oven			Till the cheese is golden brown.		

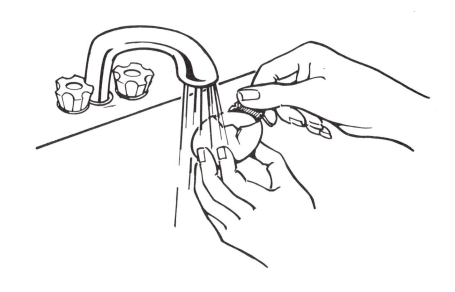

10 Eggs Baked with Chicken Livers, Bacon and Wine Sauce

Overall time:
30 min

A substantial starter. If you think it's too much, make it with only one egg each.

Process	Amount	Ingredients	Explanation	Time	Heat
1. Melt	1oz/28g	Butter	In a frying pan	1 min	Hot
2. Add and fry	2 slices	Bacon	Till crisp	2 min	Med
3. Trim and quarter	2oz/56g	Chicken Livers	Remove bacon and cook livers in the same pan for about	3 min	Med
4. De-rind the bacon			Cut in bite-size bits. Add to livers in pan	1 min	Low
5. Mix in a small bowl	2 tabls 2 tabls 1 teasp 1 teasp 1 teasp	Cold Water Wine Bisto Sugar Mustard	Preheat oven Stir well together with a wooden spoon		Med
6. Pour the wine mixture over the livers and bacon			Stir well, scraping up and mixing in the sediment. Cook, stirring for	1 min	Hot
7. Season with		Salt, Pepper	Pour into an ovenproof dish or into cocotte dishes		
8. Break into a cup	1	Egg	Slide it carefully on top of liver and bacon		
9. Repeat with another	3	Eggs	Cook in the oven	7 min	Med
10. Chop finely	2 teasp	Parsley	Sprinkle over eggs and serve at once		

11 Eggs Baked with Lettuce and Cream with Tomato Sauce

Overall time:
1 hr

Serve either hot or cold; it looks very appetizing if you surround it, on a plate, with the sauce and sprinkle it with chopped parsley.

Process	Amount	Ingredients	Explanation	Time	Heat
1. Separate leaves of	1 medium	Lettuce	Wash them well		
2. Bring to the boil	½pt/280ml	Water	Add lettuce and boil	4 min	Hot
3. Strain lettuce			Put under cold tap Squeeze dry and chop	½ min	
4. Beat	2	Eggs	With an eggbeater	1 min	
5. Add	¼pt/140ml	Cream	Beat into eggs		
6. Add	½ teasp	Salt, Pepper Nutmeg	Beat well together		
7. Add chopped lettuce			Stir well together		
8. Rub evenly	1 teasp	Butter	Over the inside of a small ovenproof dish		
9. Pour the mixture			Into the dish. Put in the oven and cook	45 min	Med
10. Meanwhile, peel and chop fine	1 small	Onion			
11. Melt	1 oz/28g	Butter	In a small saucepan	1 min	Hot
12. Add onions			Cook and stir	8 min	Med
13. Chop and add	8oz/225g	Tomatoes (1 small tin)	Squash well together with a potato masher		
14. Add	2 teasp	Salt, Pepper Basil (chopped fresh or dried)			
15. Add and stir well	1 teasp	Sugar	Cook gently for You can sieve or liquidize the sauce if you want it to be more elegant	30 min	Low

Egg Mousse with Shrimps, Apple and Celery

Overall time:
1 hr

This light first course also looks very pretty as part of a buffet; even prettier with a ring of sliced cucumber surrounding the mould. If you don't have a mould use a dish and serve the shrimp mixture separately.

Process	Amount	Ingredients	Explanation	Time	Heat
1. Boil till hard	3	Eggs	In a saucepan of water	10 min	Hot
2. Meanwhile, put	4 tabls	Water	In another little pan		
3. Add and dissolve Allow to cool. Stir in	3 teasp ½ teasp	Gelatine Tabasco (optional)	Stirring constantly for Shell the hard eggs	1 min	Med
4. Beat with egg-beater	¼pt/140ml	Cream	Till thick		
5. Add	4 tabls	Mayonnaise			
6. Add gelatine. Add		Salt, Pepper	Stir well together		
7. Mash the eggyolks well with a fork. Cut the whites roughly			Add both to the other ingredients and mix very well		
8. Put this mixture into a ring mould			Put in refrigerator. Turn out when set (if you use a dish, don't turn it out)	Approx 20 min	
9. Chop finely	2 stalks	Celery	Put in a bowl		
10. Peel and dice finely	1 eating	Apple	Add to the celery		
11. Add and stir well in	2oz/56g peeled	Shrimps (frozen or fresh)			
12. Add and stir well	2 tabls	Mayonnaise			
13. Add and stir		Salt, Pepper	Fill ring mould with this mixture		
14. Chop finely	2 teasp	Parsley	Sprinkle over mousse and serve when needed		

Eggs and Mushrooms with Sherry Sauce

Quite a substantial first course, so you should plan on a light follow-up. Or you can use only one egg per person. It is good surrounded with little triangles of toast or fried bread with the crusts cut off.

Process	Amount	Ingredients	Explanation	Time	Heat
1. Clean and slice	4oz/112g	Mushrooms			
2. Melt in a frying pan	1oz/28g	Butter	Add the mushrooms. Stir and cook for	2 min	Hot
3. Add	8 tabls	Water			
4. Add and dissolve	½	Chicken cube	Stirring constantly for	1 min	Med
5. Add and stir well	2 tabls	Sherry			
6. Season with		Salt, Pepper	Cover pan and cook	10 min	Low
7. Remove lid. Take	4	Eggs	And, one at a time, break them into a cup and then slide them into the pan		
8. Cover pan again			Cook gently for	4 min	Low
9. Chop finely	2 teasp	Parsley			
10. Transfer eggs very carefully to a serving dish			Using a large metal spoon (preferably perforated)		
11. Pour the sauce			Around the eggs		
12. Sprinkle with			Parsley and serve at once		

14 Spinach and Ham Soufflé

This soufflé is always a great success. You can do the first 9 steps early on. *If it's the first soufflé you have ever made, please read p.xv before you start.*

Process	Amount	Ingredients	Explanation	Time	Heat
1. Defrost	1 small box of frozen	Chopped Spinach	Squeeze out water		
2. Chop in tiny pieces	2oz/56g	Ham	Reserve		
3. Melt	2oz/56g	Butter	In a saucepan	½ min	Hot
4. Add	2 tabls	Plain Flour	Stir well in	½ min	Low
5. Take from heat. Add	½pt/280ml	Milk	Slowly, stirring well in		
6. Return to heat. Beat			With an eggbeater for	2 min	Hot
7. Add 4 tabls of spinach			(Keep the rest for something else.) Stir well		
8. Add the chopped ham Take off heat			Stir well together. Cook Cover pan till needed	1 min	Med
9. Separate (see p.xv)	3	Eggs	Putting whites in a mixing bowl and beating yolks into the mixture with a wooden spoon		
10. Season with	¼ teasp	Salt, Pepper Nutmeg	Preheat the oven Cover pan till needed		Hot
11. Rub evenly	1 teasp	Butter	Inside a small soufflé dish or any ovenproof dish (of about 6"/15 cm)		
12. Whip the eggwhites			With the clean, dry eggbeater till they stand up in peaks	Approx 3 min	
13. Fold *at once* with (See p.xv)			The spinach mixture using a big metal spoon		
14. Pour this mixture into prepared dish			Cook in the oven	25 min	Hot
15. Serve immediately					

Salmon and Cucumber Soufflé

Overall time:
1 hr

You can use fresh salmon for this but tinned tastes very good mixed with the subtle flavour of the cooked cucumber, seasoned with the cheese. *If this is your first attempt at making a soufflé please read p.xv.*

Process	Amount	Ingredients	Explanation	Time	Heat
1. Rub evenly	½oz/14g	Butter	Inside a 6″/15cm soufflé or oven dish		
2. Melt in a saucepan	2oz/56g	Butter			Hot
3. Add and stir well	2 tabls	Plain Flour	Remove from heat		
4. Add and stir well	½pt/280ml	Milk	Return to heat. Cook, beating constantly with an eggbeater for	2 min	Hot
5. Remove from heat			Cover pan and leave		
6. Cut in small pieces	3″/7cm	Cucumber	Preheat oven		Hot
7. Melt in a small pan	½oz/14g	Butter	Add cucumber. Stir well Cover pan and cook	2 min 5 min	Med Low
8. Open a tin of approx	5oz/140g	Salmon (1 small tin)	Remove skin and bones and break into pieces		
9. Liquidize or mash			The cooked cucumber		
10. Separate (see p.xv)	3	Eggs	Add the yolks to the milk and flour mixture (put whites in a bowl)		
11. Then add and mix well			The salmon and cucumber		
12. Grate and add	1oz/28g	Cheese			
13. Season well with		Salt, Pepper	Stir well together		
14. Using the clean, dry eggbeater			Beat the whites till they are stiff peaks	Approx 3 min	
15. Fold the mixture (see p.xv)			Into the eggwhites, pour into the prepared soufflé dish and cook in the oven	25 min	Hot
16. Serve immediately					

Gruyère and Parmesan Soufflé

Overall time:
45 min

A perfect cheese soufflé, which can be made with any cheese or combination of cheeses. *If this is your first attempt at making a soufflé please read p.xv.*

Process	Amount	Ingredients	Explanation	Time	Heat
1. Rub evenly	1 teasp	Butter	Inside a 6"/15cm soufflé or oven dish		
2. Melt in a saucepan	2oz/56g	Butter	Preheat oven		Hot
3. Add and stir	2 tabls	Plain Flour	With a wooden spoon. Remove pan from heat		
4. Add and stir well	½pt/280ml	Milk	Return to heat and beat with an eggbeater for Turn off heat	2 mins	Hot
5. Grate coarsely	3oz/84g	Cheese	Stir well in		
6. Season with	1 teasp	Salt, Pepper English or French Mustard	Stir well in		
7. Separate (see p.xv)	2	Eggs	Add the yolks to the cheese mixture and stir well in		
8. With the clean, dry eggbeater			Beat the eggwhites till they become stiff peaks	2 min	
9. Fold in (see p.xv)			The cheese mixture with the egg-whites as lightly and quickly as possible		
Sprinkle on	½ teasp	Nutmeg (optional)			
10. Pour into the prepared oven dish			Cook in the oven	25 min	Med

Haddock, or any White Fish Fillets with a Creamy Sherry Sauce

Overall time: 30 min

This sauce goes well with any fish, making the cheapest fish taste special. With sole, of course, it really *is* special.

Process	Amount	Ingredients	Explanation	Time	Heat
1. Peel and chop finely	1 small	Onion			
2. Melt	2oz/56g	Butter	In a frying pan	1 min	Hot
3. Skin and put in	2 6oz/168g	Fish fillets	Cook gently for Turn. Cook other side	3 min 3 min	Med Med
4. Using the fish slice			Move fish to a serving dish. Cover, put in oven		V.Low
5. Add onion to frying pan			Cook, stirring constantly with a wooden spoon	8 min	Low
6. Sprinkle on	2 teasp	Plain Flour	Mix well with onions		
7. Take off heat. Add	4 tabls	Milk	Mix well, return to heat. Cook, stirring constantly	2 min	Med.
8. Stir well in	2 tabls	Sherry	Cook, stirring constantly	1 min	Med
9. Season with	¼ teasp 1 teasp	Salt, Pepper Nutmeg French Mustard	Cook, stirring constantly	1 min	Med
10. Stir well in	1 tabls	Cream/Milk		½ min	Hot
11. Pour this sauce over the fish			Cover with foil. Put in oven till needed		
12. Wash and chop finely	2 teasp	Chives or Dill or Parsley	Sprinkle over the fish and serve		

Fillets of Fish Wrapped in Lettuce Leaves

Use any white fish fillets; even the cheapest tastes good like this. It is well worth the extra bit of trouble. (Using frozen chopped spinach saves time.)

Process	Amount	Ingredients	Explanation	Time	Heat
1. Wash or defrost	2oz/56g	Spinach	Cook in a saucepan for	4 min	Hot
2. Drain. Chop fine. Add	2oz/56g	Butter	Cut in bits and mix		
3. Cut crusts off	1 slice	White Bread	Crumble into spinach		
4. Season with		Salt, Pepper	Mix all well together		
5. Peel and chop	1 medium	Onion	Very finely		
6. Melt in a saucepan	1oz/28g	Butter	Add onions, cook and stir Cover pan. Leave to cook	2 min	Hot V.Low
7. Half-split	2 6oz/168g	Fish Fillets (skinned)	by using a sharp knife and cutting a lengthways slit in each fillet to make a pocket in each		
8. Sprinkle well with		Salt, Pepper Garlic Powder	Fill the slits with the spinach mixture		
9. Wash and lay flat Sprinkle with	6 1 teasp	Lettuce leaves Salt	In a saucepan (Use the big outer leaves)		
10. Pour over	¼pt/140ml	Water	Bring to the boil. Cook	2 min	Hot
11. Put in a strainer			Run cold water over the leaves. Drain, then wrap them round the fillets		
12. Rub evenly Put in the onions	½oz/14g	Butter	Inside an ovenproof dish Spread them around		
13. Season with		Salt, Pepper	Put fillets on top		
14. Pour over	4 tabls	White Wine	Cover with foil and cook in the oven for	30 min	Hot
15. Remove foil. Put in	4 tabls	Cream	Stir well with the juices in the dish. Heat in oven	3 min	Hot

Melon Halves Filled with Prawns in Lightly Curried Mayonnaise

Overall time:
20 mins

A real appetizer. You can prepare steps 1 to 5 early in the day. A wonderful cold supper or buffet dish too, made in bigger quantities and served in a bowl

Process	Amount	Ingredients	Explanation	Time	Heat
1. Cut evenly in half	1 small	Melon	Remove all the flesh, cut in bite-size cubes. Put in a strainer (keep the skins for serving)		
2. Add to the strainer	4oz/112g peeled	Prawns, Fresh or Frozen	Put strainer over a bowl and keep in the cold till 15 mins before you need it		
3. Wash and de-string	1 big stick	Celery	Chop very finely		
4. Mix with	4 tabls	Mayonnaise	In a small bowl		
5. Add and mix well	2 teasp	Curry Powder	Keep cool till needed		
6. 15 mins before meal			Combine all ingredients		
7. Sprinkle over	½ teasp ¼ teasp	Salt, Pepper Ginger Powder Tabasco	Gently mix well together		
8. Chop finely and add	2 teasp	Mint or Parsley	Mix well together		
9. Spoon this mixture			Into the two melon-half skins or a serving dish		
10. Chop finely another	2 teasp	Mint or Parsley	Sprinkle over and serve		

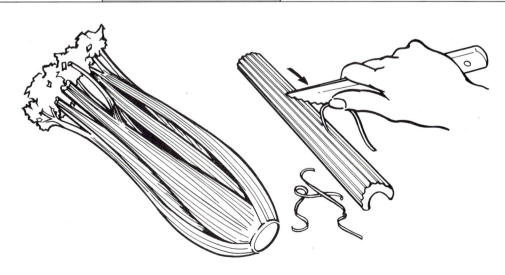

Salmon Mousse with Cold Watercress Sauce

A light starter, or cold supper dish. The crispness and slight sharpness of the green sauce goes well with the smooth mousse. If you have no ring mould, leave the mousse in the dish and serve sauce separately. A liquidizer or Mouli is essential for the sauce.

Process	Amount	Ingredients	Explanation	Time	Heat
1. Put	4 tabls	Water	In a small saucepan		
2. Add and stir well	4 teasp	Gelatine	Heat till gelatine is well dissolved	2 min	Med
3. Add and mix well in	½	Chicken cube			
4. Add and mix well	2 teasp	Tomato Puree	Allow to cool		
5. Open a tin of	7oz/225g approx.	Salmon	Remove skin and bones. Mash with a fork		
6. Beat till just thick	4 tabls	Cream	Combine all ingredients		
7. Season with	¼ teasp	Salt, Pepper Tabasco (optional)	Mix well together		
8. Separate (see p.xv)	2	Eggs	Keep yolks for something else. Beat whites till they are stiff peaks	2 min	
9. Fold whites (see p.xv)			Into the mixture using a big metal spoon		
10. Pour mixture into a dish or ring mould			Put in refrigerator. Leave to set	Approx 30 min	
11. Meanwhile, wash and chop	½ bunch	Watercress			
12. Put in a saucepan. Add	3 tabls	Water	Cover pan and cook	7 min	Med
13. Liquidize or put through a Mouli			Allow to cool		
14. Chop in small bits	3"/15cm	Cucumber	Add to watercress		
15. Stir well in	3 tabls	Mayonnaise			
16. Season with		Salt, Pepper	Keep cool till needed		
17. Turn out the salmon mousse			Fill salmon ring with green sauce		

Scallops with Mushrooms and Onions Gratinée (in their shells)

Overall time:
45 min

This can be served as a first course with little triangles of crustless toast, or as a main course with mashed potatoes and petits pois.

Process	Amount	Ingredients	Explanation	Time	Heat
1. Bring to the boil	½pt/280ml	Milk	In a saucepan		Hot
2. Cut into quarters	4 large	Scallops	Add to milk and cook for	3 min	Med
3. Remove from heat. Peel	1 medium	Onion	Chop very finely		
4. Melt in a saucepan	3oz/84g	Butter	Add onions. Cook and stir Cover pan. Lower heat. Cook	3 min 5 min	Hot Low
5. Chop quite small	4oz/112g	Mushrooms	Add to the onions. Cook, stirring constantly	3 min	Med
6. Sprinkle over	2 teasp	Plain Flour	Stir well together		Low
7. Strain milk in which scallops were cooked			Pour over the mixture. Stir well together and cook, stirring constantly	5 min	Med
8. Add scallops and		Salt, Pepper	Stir and cook gently	3 min	Low
9. Grate	1oz/28g	Cheese			
10. Pour mixture			Into an ovenproof dish or into two cocottes or two scallop shells		
11. Sprinkle cheese over the top			Brown under the grill or in the oven for about	10 min	Hot
12. Chop finely	2 teasp	Parsley	Sprinkle over and serve		

Garlic Bread Rolls Filled with Creamed Mushrooms

Overall time:
15 mins

A mouthwatering combination, quick and easy to make.

Process	Amount	Ingredients	Explanation	Time	Heat
1. Preheat the oven					Med
2. Cut the tops off	2 crispy	Rolls	Scoop out enough of the soft bread inside to make a deep hole		
3. Soften	3oz/84g	Butter	In a bowl, mashing with a fork		
4. Add and mix well	1 teasp	Chopped Garlic (fresh or dried)	Spread this mixture inside the bread rolls. Cook in oven	10 min	Med
5. Meanwhile, chop	½lb/224g	Mushrooms	In small pieces		
6. Melt	1oz/28g	Butter	In a pan, add mushrooms. Stir and cook	5 min	Hot
7. Season with	¼ teasp	Salt, Pepper Tarragon	Mix well together		
8. Add and stir well	4 tabls	Cream	Stir all together for	1 min	Hot
9. Fill the rolls			With this mixture		
10. Chop	1 teasp	Parsley	Sprinkle over and serve		

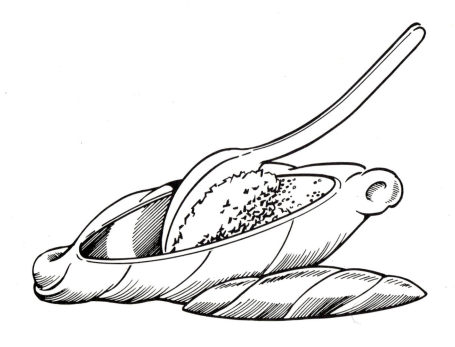

23 Stuffed Mushrooms

Overall time:
35 min

As a starter, these are best served on toast and sprinkled with parsley. Little ones can be served with the main course as a special vegetable.

Process	Amount	Ingredients	Explanation	Time	Heat
1. Peel and chop finely	1 small	Onion	Preheat oven		Hot
2. Melt in a saucepan	1oz/28g	Butter	Add onions. Fry and stir Cover pan, lower heat	2 min 5 min	Hot Low
3. Meanwhile, put	2 4 large	Horse mushrooms or ordinary Mushrooms	On a baking tray, with the gills facing down		
4. Rub over their skins	1 tabls	Oil	Put in the oven for	7 min	Hot
5. Remove crusts from	1 slice	White Bread	Crumble over onions in saucepan. Stir and cook	2 min	Hot
6. Add and stir well	2 tabls 3 teasp ½	Water Tomato Puree Chicken cube			
7. Chop and stir well in	2 teasp	Parsley	Cook together for about	3 min	Low
8. Season with		Salt, Pepper			
9. Take off heat. Add	½ teasp	Garlic (fresh or powder)	Mix well together. Cover pan and leave till needed.		
10. Remove baking tray from oven			Turn mushrooms over. Pile tomato and bread mixture on top		
11. Divide into lumps	½oz/14g	Butter	Put a lump on top of each mushroom. Put back in the oven and cook for	10 min	Med
12. Cut crusts off	2 slices	Bread	Toast bread. Put mushrooms on top		
13. Chop finely	2 teasp	Parsley	Sprinkle over and serve		

24 Endives Wrapped in Ham with a White Sauce Gratinée

Overall time:
45 min

Best made with Gruyère cheese, but any cheese will do. It makes a good light lunch or supper dish.

Process	Amount	Ingredients	Explanation	Time	Heat
1. Bring to the boil Add Add	½pt/280ml ½ teasp 1 teasp	Water Salt Lemon Juice	In a saucepan	2 min	Hot
2. Wash, trim and add Halve and add	4 small or 2 big	Endives Endives	Bring to the boil again Lower heat and cook	1 min 10 min	Hot Med
3. Meanwhile, melt	1oz/28g	Butter	In a saucepan	½ min	Hot
4. Add and stir well	3 teasp	Plain Flour	Take pan off heat		
5. Add and stir well	½pt/280ml	Milk	With a wooden spoon		
6. Return to heat. Add		Salt, Pepper	Beat with an eggbeater	3 min	Hot
7. Grate and add	½oz/14g	Cheese	Stir well in	1 min	Med
8. Stir well in	¼ teasp	Nutmeg	Cover pan and leave		V.Low
9. Drain the endives			In a strainer		
10. Cut in halves	2 slices	Ham	Wrap a piece of ham around each endive		
11. Rub evenly	1 teasp	Butter	Inside an ovenproof dish. Put in the endives		
12. Pour the sauce			Over the endives		
13. Grate over the top	½oz/14g	Cheese	Cook in the oven till golden brown	20 min	Hot

25   Aubergines Stuffed with Tomato and Mozzarella or Sliced Cheese

Overall time:
1½ hr

A satisfying starter, so have a light follow-up. The aubergines can be served either hot or cold, with crispy French bread.

Process	Amount	Ingredients	Explanation	Time	Heat
1. Wash and trim	1 large	Aubergine	Cut in half		
2. Bring to the boil Add	½pt/280ml ½ teasp	Water Salt	Add the aubergine Cook for	5 min	Hot
3. Drain well			In a strainer		
4. Chop finely	1 medium	Onion	Preheat oven		Med
5. Heat in a saucepan	1 tabls	Olive Oil	Add onions. Cook and stir	5 min	Low
6. Chop small and add	½lb/225g	Tomatoes (1 small tin)			Low
7. Season with	 1 teasp 1 teasp	Salt, Pepper Sugar Garlic (fresh or powder)			
8. Chop finely and add	2 teasp	Parsley	Stir well together		
9. Add and stir well in	2 teasp	Basil	Cover pan and cook for	10 min	Med
10. Put aubergines with	1 tabls	Oil	In an ovenproof dish, skin-side down. Make 4 deep slits in the flesh of each		
11. Sprinkle with		Salt, Pepper	Fill slits with the tomato mixture. Put in oven	30 min	Med
12. Put on aubergines	2 slices (approx 2oz/56g per slice)	Mozzarella or sliced cheese	Return to oven for	30 min	Low
13. Chop finely	2 teasp	Parsley	Sprinkle over and serve		

Spring Onion Quiche

Overall time:
1¼ hr

An unusual, appetizing quiche, which looks nice when you cut it and see the mixture of yellow and green. Keep a few little bits of the chopped green to sprinkle over the top when you serve it. Steps 1 to 5 can be circumvented by using 3oz frozen shortcrust pastry, rolled thin.

Process	Amount	Ingredients	Explanation	Time	Heat
1. Put in a bowl	4 tabls	Plain Flour	Preheat the oven		Hot
2. Cut over the flour	1oz/28g	Butter	In tiny bits		
3. Add	½ teasp	Salt	Rub all together very quickly and lightly with your fingertips till it is like crumbs	2 min	
4. Add and mix in	3 teasp	Cold Water	With a knife		
5. Sprinkle	½ teasp	Plain Flour	Into an 8"/20 cm flan dish or cake tin. Shake all around the bottom		
6. Put the pastry mix in the dish or tin			Dip your fingers in flour and lightly press pastry all over base into corners and up sides		
7. Prick with a fork			Cook in the oven for	15 min	Hot
8. Meanwhile, wash and trim well	2 bunches	Spring Onions	Chop them very finely		
9. Melt	1oz/28g	Butter	In a saucepan	½ min	Hot
10. Add onions and add	1	Chicken cube	Stir well. Cover and cook	15 min	V.Low
11. Meanwhile, beat in a bowl	3	Eggs	With an eggbeater for	2 min	
12. Add	¼pt/140ml	Cream	Beat into eggs		
13. Add the onions and		Salt, Pepper	Mix all well together		
14. Fill the flan case			With this mixture		
15. Grate over the top	1oz/28g	Cheese	Cook in the oven for	25 min	Hot

Stuffed Courgettes

Overall time:
45 mins

These savoury boats make an excellent starter and look very tempting sprinkled with fresh chopped basil or parsley, but they can also be served as an accompanying vegetable and are especially good with steak or chops.

Process	Amount	Ingredients	Explanation	Time	Heat
1. Cut the ends off	4 medium	Courgettes	Wash them		
2. Bring to the boil	½pt/280ml	Water	Add courgettes and cook	5 min	Hot
3. Drain them in strainer			Put under cold running water	½ min	
4. Drain and cut them in halves			Scrape the seed centres into a saucepan with a spoon		
5. Lay the halves			In an ovenproof dish green sides down		
6. Add to the saucepan	1oz/28g	Butter	Cook the centres, stirring constantly	5 min	Med
7. Mash well			With a potato masher or fork Take pan off the heat		
8. Sprinkle and stir in	4 teasp	Plain Flour			
9. Add and stir well in	¼pt/140ml	Milk	Return pan to heat and cook, stirring constantly	3 min	Hot
10. Grate and add	2oz/56g	Cheese	Mix well together		
11. Season with		Salt, Pepper	Mix well together		
12. Add and stir well in Chop finely and add	½ teasp 1 teasp	Basil Parsley	Pile this mixture into the courgette halves		
13. Grate	1oz/28g	Cheese	Sprinkle over the tops and cook in the oven till brown	20 min	Hot

Spaghetti with Tuna Fish and Olives in Tomato Sauce

Overall time: 40 min

Quick and easy to prepare, this makes a most satisfying meal with a salad, cheese and fruit.

Process	Amount	Ingredients	Explanation	Time	Heat
1. Peel and chop finely	1 medium	Onion			
2. Melt in a saucepan	2oz/56g	Butter	Using a wooden spoon	1 min	Hot
3. Add the onions and		Salt, Pepper	Cook, stirring constantly	8 min	Med
4. Chop and add	½lb/225g	Tomatoes (1 small tin)	Stir well together		
5. Add and stir well	2 teasp / 1 teasp	Basil / Sugar	Cover pan and cook	10 min	Low
6. Meanwhile, boil	4pt/2lt	Water	In a large saucepan		Hot
7. When boiling, add	½lb/225g / 4 teasp	Spaghetti / Salt	Stir immediately and well, making sure the strands are all separated. Boil	8–12 min	Med
8. Meanwhile, open a tin of	4oz/112g	Tuna Fish (1 small tin)	Flake it. Add to the tomato sauce		Low
9. Remove stones from	10	Black Olives	Add to the sauce and mix well together		Low
10. Pour the spaghetti			Into a strainer and put under the hot tap	½ min	
11. Put spaghetti in a serving dish			Pour tomato sauce over it		
12. Chop finely	2 teasp	Parsley	Sprinkle over and serve		

Tortellini with Tomato and Basil Sauce

Overall time:
40 min

Simple and traditional. Fresh parmesan is the best grated cheese to serve with it, and a mixed salad on the side.

Process	Amount	Ingredients	Explanation	Time	Heat
1. Peel and chop finely	1 large	Onion			
2. Melt in a saucepan	2oz/56g	Butter	Using a wooden spoon	1 min	Hot
3. Add the onions and		Salt, Pepper	Cook, stirring constantly	8 min	Med
4. Chop and add	1lb/450g	Tomatoes (1 medium tin)	Stir well together		
5. Add and stir well in	1 2 teasp 1 teasp 3 teasp	Bayleaf Sugar Garlic (fresh or powder) Basil (fresh if possible)			
6. Add and stir well in	1 teasp	Paprika	Cover saucepan and cook	30 min	Low
7. Meanwhile, boil	2pt/1lt	Water	In a large saucepan		Hot
8. Put in	½lb/225g	Tortellini	Stir immediately to make sure pasta is separated		Hot
9. Add and stir well	3 teasp	Salt	Lower heat and cook for	10 min	Med
10. Grate finely	4oz/112g	Cheese	Put in a small bowl and keep to serve at table		
11. Drain the tortellini in a strainer			Put it in a serving dish and pour the tomato sauce over it		
12. Chop finely	2 teasp	Basil or Parsley	Sprinkle over and serve		

Tagliatelli with Creamy Ham Sauce

Overall time:
25 min

Freshly grated parmesan is much the best, if you can afford it, but any cheese will do. It's good with a white wine and a green salad.

Process	Amount	Ingredients	Explanation	Time	Heat
1. Put to boil	4pt/2lt	Water	In a large saucepan		Hot
2. Meanwhile, chop in little bits	6oz/168g	Cooked Ham	Keep till needed		
3. Melt	2oz/56g	Butter	In a saucepan		Hot
4. Add and stir	1 tabls	Plain Flour	With a wooden spoon		
5. Take off heat and add	½pt/280ml	Milk	Stir well together		
6. Return to heat			Beat with an eggbeater	2 min	Hot
7. Add and stir well in	½ teasp	Salt, Pepper Grated Nutmeg (optional)	Add the chopped ham. Mix well in. Cover pan		V.Low
8. Add to the boiling water	½lb/225g 4 teasp	Tagliatelli and Salt	Stir immediately, making sure the strands are separate		
9. Bring back to the boil			Lower heat and cook until tender	5–8 min	Med
10. Pour the tagliatelli into a strainer			Put under the hot running water	½ min	
11. Put in a dish. Add		Pepper	Pour the ham sauce over the top		
12. Chop finely	2 teasp	Parsley	Sprinkle over		
13. Serve with	2oz/56g	Grated Cheese	In a separate dish to spoon over the top		

31 Pasta Shapes with a Mixed Vegetable Sauce

Overall time:
1 hr

You can use any vegetables you like in this mixture (add lots of garlic if you want a stronger sauce), and any kind of pasta shapes: shells, butterflies, spirals, or just ordinary spaghetti or noodles.

Process	Amount	Ingredients	Explanation	Time	Heat
1. Peel and chop finely	1 medium	Onion			
2. Melt	1oz/28g	Butter	In a saucepan	½ min	Hot
3. Add the onions and	1 teasp	Garlic	Cook and stir for	5 min	Hot
4. Scrape and chop	1 medium	Carrot	Add to the onions. Cook	3 mins	Hot
5. Remove strings from	1 stick	Celery	Chop small and add		Med
6. Remove seeds from	½	Green Pepper	Chop small and add		Med
7. Trim and slice fine	1 medium	Courgette	Stir in		Med
8. Chop small and add	½lb/225g	Tomatoes (1 small tin)			Med
9. Season well with		Salt, Pepper			
	1 teasp	Sugar	Bring to the boil. Stir	2 min	Hot
	2 teasp	Mixed Herbs	Cover pan and cook	40 min	Low
10. Bring to the boil	3pt/1½lt	Water	In a large saucepan		Hot
11. Add	3 teasp	Salt			
12. Add	½lb/225g	Pasta Shapes	Stir immediately, making sure the pasta is separated. Boil for	10 min	Med
13. Meanwhile, grate	4oz/112g	Cheese	Put in a small bowl and keep to serve at the table		
14. Drain the pasta in a strainer			Put it in a serving dish and pour the sauce over it		
15. Chop	2 teasp	Parsley	Sprinkle over the top and serve		

Macaroni with Pink Béchamel Sauce, Diced Ham and Courgettes

Overall time:
40 min

Courgettes are optional, but their addition makes a more unusual and attractive way to serve Penne (or short-cut macaroni). As always with pasta, freshly grated parmesan is the best cheese, if possible.

Process	Amount	Ingredients	Explanation	Time	Heat
1. Bring to the boil	3pt/1½lt	Water	In a large saucepan		Hot
2. Add	½lb/225g	Penne (Short Macaroni)	Stir immediately, making sure the pasta is separated.	Approx	
	3 teasp	Salt	Cook until tender	12 min	Med
3. Wash, slice and add	2 medium	Courgettes	Stir well in		
4. Meanwhile, put	1 tabls	Cornflour	Into a bowl		
5. Pour in and stir well	½pt/280ml	Milk	With a wooden spoon		
6. Add	¼ teasp	Tabasco	Stir well together		
7. Melt in a saucepan	2oz/56g	Butter	Add the milk mixture. Cook, stirring constantly	3 min	Hot
8. Lower heat. Put	3 teasp	Tomato Puree	In a small bowl		
9. Add and mix well	3 tabls	Milk	Stir into sauce and cook	2 min	Hot
10. Lower heat and add		Salt, Pepper	Mix well in. Cover pan		V.Low
11. Cut in small pieces	6oz/168g	Ham	Mix with sauce. Re-cover		V.Low
12. Drain macaroni and courgette mixture			In a strainer		
13. Put in a serving dish			Pour the sauce over and mix well together. (You can cover the dish and keep it warm in the oven if necessary)		V.Low
14. Grate finely	2oz/56g	Cheese	Put in a small bowl and serve separately with the pasta		

33 Macaroni with Meat Baked with a Cheese Sauce

Overall time:
1½ hr

This makes a good, satisfying lunch dish or dinner dish for a casual after-the-cinema evening. You can leave it in a very low oven for quite a while. Serve it with salad.

Process	Amount	Ingredients	Explanation	Time	Heat
1. Peel and chop finely	1 large	Onion			
2. Heat in a saucepan	2 tabls	Oil	Add onions. Cook and stir	5 min	Hot
3. Add	½lb/225g	Minced Beef	Stir with a wooden spoon. Cook, stirring occasionally	5 min	Hot
4. Chop small	½lb/225g	Tomatoes (1 small tin)	Add to the meat and stir well together		
5. Season with	1 teasp 1 teasp 1 teasp 2 teasp	Salt, Pepper Sugar Garlic (fresh or powder) Paprika Mixed Herbs	Mix well together		
6. Add	1	Bayleaf	Cover pan and cook	30 min	Low
7. Meanwhile, boil	3pt/1½lt	Water	In a large saucepan		Hot
8. Break in bite-size bits	½lb/225g	Macaroni	Put into the water		
9. Add	4 teasp	Salt	Stir immediately, making sure pasta is separated. Cook	10 min	Med
10. Pour into a strainer			Put under a hot tap for	½ min	
11. Put macaroni with		Salt, Pepper	In an ovenproof dish		
12. Melt in a small pan	2oz/56g	Butter	Using a wooden spoon	1 min	Hot
13. Take off heat. Add	1 tabls	Flour	Stir well together		
14. Add and stir well	½pt/280ml	Milk Salt, Pepper	Return to heat and beat with an eggbeater for	2 min	Hot
15. Grate and add	1oz/28g	Cheese	Stir well together	2 min	Med
16. Mix the meat sauce with the macaroni			Cover with cheese sauce		
17. Grate over the top	1oz/28g	Cheese	Put in oven and cook	30 min	Hot

Pancakes Stuffed with Mushrooms

Overall time:
40 min

Process	Amount	Ingredients	Explanation	Time	Heat
1. Put	4 tabls	Plain Flour	In a bowl. Preheat oven		V.Low
2. Mix in	¼ teasp	Salt	Make a hole in the centre of the flour		
3. Break in	1	Egg	Start stirring		
4. Meanwhile adding	¼pt/140ml	Milk	Slowly, until all the flour is mixed well in		
Add extra	2 tabls	Milk	Beat with an eggbeater	3 min	
5. Melt	½ teasp	Butter	In a frying pan	½ min	Hot
6. Take pan off heat			Add about 2 tabls of mixture (enough to thinly cover the bottom) tipping the pan to allow the mixture to run evenly all over the bottom. Return to heat and cook	1 min	Hot
7. Using a fish slice			Carefully turn the pancake over and cook for	½ min	Med
8. Put the pancake on a plate			Cover and keep warm in the oven		V.Low
9. Repeat this procedure			To make 4 or 5 pancakes		
10. Chop very small	8oz/225g	Mushrooms			
11. Melt	1oz/28g	Butter	In a small pan. Add the mushrooms. Cook and stir	5 min	Hot
12. Sprinkle over	2 tabls	Flour	Stir well together		V.Low
13. Add, stir and boil	½pt/280ml	Milk	Cook, stirring constantly	3 min	Med
14. Season well with		Salt, Pepper	Spread each pancake with mushroom mixture, roll up and serve		

Creamy Rice with Smoked Fish and Chives

You can make this with any smoked fish (I usually use haddock) and add hard-boiled eggs and/or a teaspoonful of curry powder at the last minute if you like.

**Overall time:
40 min**

Process	Amount	Ingredients	Explanation	Time	Heat
1. Peel and chop finely	1 medium	Onion			
2. Melt	1oz/28g	Butter	In a saucepan	½ min	Hot
3. Add the onions			Cook, stirring constantly	5 min	Hot
4. Add and stir	4oz/112g	Rice	Stir constantly	1 min	Med
5. Pour on and stir	½pt/280ml	Water	Bring to the boil	2 min	Hot
6. Add and stir	½ teasp	Salt	Cover pan and cook. Turn off heat and leave pan covered	10 min	Low
7. Meanwhile, put	12oz/337g	Smoked Fish	In a frying pan		
8. Pour over	½pt/280ml	Milk	Cover frying pan. Cook	10 min	Med
9. Take off heat. Put fish on a plate			Skin, bone and flake it		
10. Strain the milk into the rice			Stir well. Cover, and return to heat	5 min	Med
11. Meanwhile, chop finely	4 teasp	Chives or Spring Onion tops			
12. Cut thin	4 slices	Lemon			
13. Cut in slices	1	Tomato			
14. Take rice off heat			Carefully stir in the fish and 3 teasp chives		
15. Season with	Plenty of	Pepper			
16. Add, if necessary		Salt	(Depending on the saltiness of the fish)		
17. Cover pan and leave			To stand	5 min	
18. Pile it on a dish			Decorate with the lemon and tomato slices and 1 teasp chives		

Rice with Chicken Livers and Bacon in Wine Sauce

Quick, easy and delicious. You should use red wine but failing that use white (or even water and a chicken cube). Serve with peas or green beans and a green salad.

Process	Amount	Ingredients	Explanation	Time	Heat
1. Bring to the boil Add	½pt/280ml ½ teasp	Water Salt	In a saucepan	2 min	Hot
2. Add and stir well	4oz/112g	Rice	Cover pan and boil Turn off heat and leave covered for	12 min 5 min	Low
3. Meanwhile, clean, trim	4oz/112g	Chicken Livers	Cut in bite-size bits		
4. De-rind	4 slices	Bacon	Cut in bite-size bits		
5. Heat	1 teasp	Oil	In a frying pan	½ min	Hot
6. Add and melt	1 teasp	Butter	Add bacon. Fry and stir	2 min	Med
7. Add chicken livers			Cook and stir till brown	2 min	Hot
8. Add and stir		Salt, Pepper	Cook, stirring constantly Cover and leave	2 min 3 min	Low V.Low
9. Meanwhile, put Add	4 teasp ¼pt/140ml 2 teasp 1 teasp	Bisto Wine Sugar English Mustard	In a small bowl Mix well together		
10. Add and stir well	4 tabls	Water	Pour this mixture over livers and bacon and stir very well, scraping all the bits from the base of the pan and stirring all together as sauce thickens	2 min	Hot
11. Lower heat			Cover and cook, stirring occasionally	5 min	Low
12. Mound rice onto a dish			Pour the liver mixture on top		
13. Chop finely	2 teasp	Parsley	Sprinkle over and serve		

Potatoes with Cucumber, Minced Meat and Béchamel Gratinée

Overall time:
1½ hr

An excellent dish for after-cinema supper or weekend lunch, as you can keep it in the oven. Serve with a salad.

Process	Amount	Ingredients	Explanation	Time	Heat
1. Peel and chop	1 medium	Onion			
2. Heat in a saucepan	1 tabls	Oil	Add onions and stir	3 min	Hot
3. Add and stir	½lb/225g	Minced Beef	Cook, stirring occasionally	3 min	Hot
4. Add and stir well	½pt/140ml	Water	Bring to the boil	1 min	Hot
5. Add and stir well	1½ tabls	Tomato Puree			Low
6. Season with		Salt, Pepper			
	1 teasp	Mixed Herbs	Stir, cover pan and cook	15 min	Low
7. Cut in slices	12in/30cm	Cucumber	¼in/½cm thick		
8. Heat in a frying pan	1oz/28g	Oil	Fry the cucumber slices till golden	3 min	Med
9. Using a fish slice			Remove them and put to drain in a strainer		
10. Peel and slice	2 large	Potatoes	¼in/½cm thick		
11. Fry till golden			(Add a little oil if necessary) in the same pan	3 min	Med
12. In an ovenproof dish			Put layers of these three things. Cover base with potatoes, then meat, then cucumber ending with a layer of potatoes		
13. Melt in a saucepan	1oz/28g	Butter		1 min	Hot
14. Add and stir well	2 tabls	Flour	Take off heat		
15. Add and stir well	¾pt/420ml	Milk	Beat with an eggbeater	3 min	Hot
16. Grate and mix in Stir in	2oz/56g	Cheese Salt, Pepper	Pour this over the other ingredients in the dish		
17. Grate over the top	1oz/28g	Cheese	Put in oven and cook	45 min	Med

Minced Beef and Potato Pie

Overall time:
1½ hr

My version of cottage pie. I always serve it with petits pois and a plain green salad. Worcestershire sauce is a good accompaniment.

Process	Amount	Ingredients	Explanation	Time	Heat
1. Peel and chop	1 large	Onion			
2. Melt in a frying pan	1oz/28g	Butter	Add onions and cook stirring constantly	5 min	Med
3. Chop and mix in	½lb/225g	Tomatoes (1 small tin)	Cook	5 min	Med
4. While cooking, add		Salt, Pepper	Mix well in		
5. Scrape and grate in	1 medium	Carrot	Stir in		
6. Chop very finely	1 stick	Celery	Stir in		
7. Remove seeds and chop	½	Green Pepper	Stir in		
8. Stir in	1 teasp 2 ½ teasp 1 teasp	Mixed Herbs Bay Leaves Tabasco (optional) Paprika	Cover and lower heat		Low
9. Meanwhile, put in a saucepan	¾lb/337g	Minced Beef	Cook and stir	3 min	Hot
10. Add the tomato mixture to the meat			Mix well together, cover and cook, stirring occasionally	30 min	Low
11. Meanwhile, peel	2 large	Potatoes	Cut in slices and put in a saucepan		
12. Cover potatoes with		Water	Bring to the boil. Cook till tender	Approx 20 min	Med
13. Drain off water add		Salt, Pepper	Mash potatoes with a potato masher		
14. Add and stir well	4 tabls	Milk	With a wooden spoon		
15. Add and beat well	1oz	Butter	With a wooden spoon		
16. Pour meat mixture			Into an ovenproof dish		
17. Spread potatoes			Over the top		
18. Grate over potatoes	2oz/56g	Cheese	Cook in the oven	30 min	Hot

6. Green Beans with Celery Sticks and Spring Onions
See recipe 86

Potato Pie with Minced Lamb and Aubergine

My version of the famous Greek Moussaka. Serve with a green salad, followed by grapes and cheese. If you want a richer dish, use cream instead of milk at stage 16.

Overall time:
2¼ hr

Process	Amount	Ingredients	Explanation	Time	Heat
1. Peel and chop	1 medium	Onion			
2. Melt in a saucepan	1oz/28g	Butter	Add onions and cook	5 min	Med
3. Add	½lb/225g	Minced Lamb Shoulder	Cook and stir	10 min	Hot
4. Add and stir well	½pt/280ml	Water	Scraping any bits from the base of the pan	2 min	Hot
5. Season with	½ teasp 1 teasp ½ teasp	Salt, Pepper Cinnamon Sugar Garlic (fresh or dried)	Stir in		Med
6. Add and stir well	1½ tabls	Tomato Puree	Cover pan and cook	30 min	Low
7. Meanwhile, trim and slice	1 large	Aubergine	In slices of approx ¼"/½cm		
8. Heat	1 tabls	Oil	In a frying pan	½ min	Hot
9. Add and fry			Slices until golden	Approx 3 min	Med
10. Sprinkle on a little		Salt	Put in a strainer		
11. Peel and slice	2 medium	Potatoes	Approx ¼"/½cm		
12. Heat	½ tabls	Oil	In the same frying pan	½ min	Hot
13. Add potato slices			Fry till golden	Approx 4 min	Med
14. In an oven dish			Put layers of the three things. Cover base with potatoes, then meat, then aubergines, finishing with potatoes		
15. Break into a bowl	2	Eggs	Beat with an eggbeater	2 min	
16. Add and mix well	½pt/280ml	Milk			
17. Grate and mix well	3oz/84g	Cheese			
18. Mix well in		Salt, Pepper	Pour over potatoes and cook in the oven	45 min	Med

White Beans with Pork, Bacon and Sausage

An inexpensive and easy version of the famous Cassoulet, perfect for after-cinema as it will keep in a low oven.

**Overall time:
3 hr**

Process	Amount	Ingredients	Explanation	Time	Heat
1. Put	1½ pt/840ml	Cold Water	In a saucepan		
2. Wash and add	8oz/224g	White Dried Beans	Bring to the boil. Cover. Lower heat, Leave to cook	4 min	Hot Low
3. After 1 hour, melt	½oz/14g	Butter	In a frying pan	½ min	Hot
4. Cut in bite-size bits	12oz/337g	Pork Belly	Add to the butter. Fry till golden	Approx 3 mins	Hot
5. De-rind and cut in bite-size bits	4 slices	Bacon	Fry with pork. Remove both and keep	2 min	Med
6. Peel, chop and add	1 medium	Onion	Cook, stirring constantly	3 min	Med
7. Add and stir well	½pt/280ml	Water	Scraping all the bits from the base of the pan		
8. Add and stir well	½ tabls	Tomato Puree			
9. Season with	1 teasp 1 teasp 3 1 1 teasp	Salt, Pepper Sugar Mixed Herbs Cloves Bay Leaf Garlic (fresh or dried)	Stir. Add this mixture to the beans and stir in		
10. Stir well in	4 tabls	Wine (optional)	Add the meat and bacon and mix with beans. Cover and continue cooking	20 min	Low
11. Cut in bite size bits	½	Boiling-ring Garlic Sausage	Add to the beans. Mix. Cover and continue cooking till the liquid has nearly gone and the beans and meat are tender. Put in a bowl		Low
12. Chop finely	2 tabls	Parsley	Mix half with the beans sprinkle the rest over and serve.		

Potatoes with Anchovies and Onions

This was given to me by a Swedish friend. In Sweden it is called Jensen's Temptation. You can serve it on its own with a salad, or as an accompaniment to, e.g. cold chicken or poached eggs.

Overall time:
1½ hr

Process	Amount	Ingredients	Explanation	Time	Heat
1. Peel and chop finely	1 medium	Onion			
2. Melt in a frying pan	½oz/14g	Butter	Add the onions and cook stirring constantly	5 min	Med
3. Season with	Pinch of 1 teasp	Salt, Pepper Dill (optional)			
4. Peel and slice	2 large	Potatoes	Cut them in half lengthways and then in slices of about ¼in/½cm		
5. Open a tin of approx	2oz/56g	Anchovies	Pour away oil		
6. Put in layers i.e.			Line an oven dish with potatoes, add a layer of onions then add anchovies. Finish with potatoes		
7. Cut in tiny bits	¼oz/7g	Butter	Over the top. Heat oven		Hot
8. Pour over	¼pt/140ml	Milk/Cream	Cook in the oven	1 hr	Hot

Smoked Fish Pie

Overall time:
1 hr

Process	Amount	Ingredients	Explanation	Time	Heat
1. Peel and slice	2 large	Potatoes	Put in a saucepan		
2. Cover with water, add	2 teasp	Salt	Boil. Lower heat. Cook	20 min	Med
3. Meanwhile, put	½pt/280ml	Milk	In a saucepan. Cook	1 min	Hot
4. Add to the milk	12oz/337g	Smoked Fish	Cover the saucepan and cook gently for	5 min	Low
5. Take fish from milk			Bone, skin and flake it (keep milk for sauce). Put fish in an ovenproof dish in the oven		V.Low
6. In a small pan, put	2	Eggs	Cover with water and boil	10 min	Hot
7. Peel and chop finely	1 medium	Onion			
8. Melt in another pan	2oz/56g	Butter	Add onions. Fry and stir	8 min	Med
9. Remove from heat. Add	1 tabls	Plain Flour	Mix well together		
10. Pour on the milk the fish was cooked in			Bring to the boil and cook, stirring constantly	5 min	Hot
11. Shell the eggs under a cold tap			Cut in quarters and add them to the sauce. Lower heat		Low
12. Drain potatoes. Add	4 tabls 1oz/28g	Milk Butter Salt, Pepper	Mash, with a potato masher or a fork and beat well together		
13. Pour egg sauce over the fish			Mix well in. Spread potatoes over the top		
14. Make 12 slices of	2 medium	Tomatoes	Place on top. Cook in the oven	20 min	Hot

Crab or Prawn Flan

You can use either to equally good effect. (Frozen crab-sticks taste really special.)
Serve as a main course with a green salad, or as a starter.

Overall time:
1 hr

Process	Amount	Ingredients	Explanation	Time	Heat
1. Put in a bowl	4 tabls	Flour	Preheat the oven		Med
2. Cut over the flour	1oz/28g	Butter	In tiny bits		
3. Add	½ teasp	Salt	Rub all together very quickly and lightly with your fingertips till it is like crumbs	2 min	
4. Mix in	3 teasp	Cold Water	With a knife		
5. Sprinkle	½ teasp	Flour	Into a 8"/20cm flan dish (or cake tin) shake all round bottom and sides		
6. Put the pastry mix in the dish			Dip your fingers in flour and lightly press pastry all over base into corners and up sides		
7. Prick with a fork			Cook in the oven	15 min	Hot
8. Peel and chop	1 small	Onion			
9. Melt in a saucepan	1oz/28g	Butter	Add onions. Cook and stir	8 min	Med
10. Chop small and add	2oz/56g	Mushrooms	Cook, stirring constantly	3 mins	Hot
11. Sprinkle over	2 teasp	Flour	Mix well. Take off heat		
12. Add	¼pt/140ml	Milk	Return to heat, stir constantly	3 min	Med
13. Break into a bowl	2	Eggs	Beat with an eggbeater	2 min	
14. Add the eggs to the mixture					
15. Season with		Salt, Pepper	Mix all together		
16. Add	4 chopped or 4oz/112g	Crab Sticks Prawns	Mix all carefully		
17. Pour into flan case			Cook in the oven	25 min	Hot
18. Chop finely	2 teasp	Chives or Parsley	Sprinkle over and serve		

44   Fillets of Fish with Grapes, Wine and Parsley Sauce

Overall time:
45 min

This is best made with fillets of sole and served with baby new potatoes tossed in butter and chopped mint and green beans, petits pois or courgettes.

Process	Amount	Ingredients	Explanation	Time	Heat
1. Peel and de-pip	4oz/112g	Grapes	Keep in a bowl		
2. Melt in a saucepan	2oz/56g	Butter	Using a wooden spoon	1 min	Hot
3. Add and stir well	2 tabls	Flour	Remove from heat		
4. Add and stir well	½pt/280ml	Milk	Return to heat and beat with an eggbeater for	2 min	Hot
5. Season with		Salt, Pepper	Preheat oven		Hot
6. Add and stir well	3 tabls	White Wine	Remove from heat, add the grapes and mix well		
7. Rub evenly	2 teasp	Butter	Inside an ovenproof dish		
8. Roll up or lay side by side	4 fillets (approx 3oz/112g each)	Fish	In the ovenproof dish		
9. Chop finely	1 tabls	Parsley	Stir into sauce		
10. Stir into sauce	2oz/56g	Frozen Shrimps (optional)	Pour sauce over fish		
11. Cover the dish			Cook in the oven	20 min	Hot

45 Prawns with Tomato, Pimento and Orange Sauce

Overall time:
45 min

Serve this on a bed of plain boiled rice with peas or french beans.

Process	Amount	Ingredients	Explanation	Time	Heat
1. Peel and chop	1 medium	Onion			
2. Melt in a saucepan	2oz/56g	Butter	Add onions and cook, stirring constantly Lower heat and cover pan	5 min	Med V.Low
3. De-seed and chop finely	½	Red Pepper	Add to onions. Cook	2 min	Med
4. Chop and stir in	½lb/225g	Tomatoes (1 small tin)			Med
5. Stir in	¼pt/140ml	White Wine			
6. Season with	½ teasp	Salt, Pepper Tabasco	Cover and cook	20 min	Low
7. Liquidize or sieve this mixture			Return it to saucepan		
8. Stir in	½ teasp	Bovril			
9. Squeeze	½	Orange	Add juice to the mixture		
10. Chop finely and stir in	2 teasp	Orange rind		2 min	Low
11. Stir in	8oz/225g	Peeled Prawns (frozen or fresh)			Med
12. Chop fine and add	1 teasp	Parsley	Stir	1 min	Hot
13. Stir in	1 tabls	Brandy (optional)			
14. Chop finely	2 teasp	Parsley	Sprinkle on top and serve		

Monkfish or Scallops and Bacon with Sherry and Cream

**Overall time:
20 min**

Serve with plain boiled rice or surrounded with lightly mashed potatoes, or new potatoes, and courgettes or french beans – or just with crispy french bread.

Process	Amount	Ingredients	Explanation	Time	Heat
1. Put in a pan	12oz/337g or 6	Monkfish fillet Scallops			
2. Pour in	3 tabls	Water	Bring to the boil	1 min	Hot
3. Lower heat and add	¼ teasp 1	Salt Bayleaf	Cover pan and cook	6 min	Low
4. Meanwhile, put in a frying pan	2 slices	Bacon	Fry till crisp. Remove from pan, cut off rind and chop small	3 min	Med
5. Drain fish or scallops			Cut in bite-size bits		
6. Melt in a saucepan	1oz/28g	Butter	Add the bacon and fish	1 min	Hot
7. Pour in	2 tabls	Sherry	Stir well, lower heat	2 min	Low
8. Stir in	4 tabls	Cream			
9. Season with		Salt, Pepper	Bring almost to the boil — *do not* allow to boil	½ min	Hot
10. Stir in	½ teasp	Nutmeg	Turn off heat. Cover pan	2 min	
11. Chop finely	2 teasp	Parsley	Sprinkle on top and serve		

Fillets of Fish with Pink Shrimp Sauce

**Overall time:
40 min**

You can use any fish for this; I usually make it with cod or monkfish. It is best served with little new potatoes tossed in butter and french beans or petits pois and a cucumber salad.

Process	Amount	Ingredients	Explanation	Time	Heat
1. Chop very finely	1 medium	Onion			
2. Melt in a saucepan	½oz	Butter	Using a wooden spoon	1 min	Hot
3. Add the onions			Cook and stir	5 min	Med
4. Stir in	¼pt/140ml	White Wine	Cover pan and cook	15 min	Med
5. Meanwhile, put	2 each about 7oz/196g	Fish Fillets	In a frying pan		
6. Season with		Salt, Pepper			
7. Cover fish with	½pt/280g	Milk	Cover pan and cook	10 min	Med
8. Using a fish slice			Put fish in an ovenproof dish		
9. Remove skin or bones. Keep the milk			Cover dish. Put in oven		V.Low
10. Meanwhile, melt	2oz/56g	Butter	In a small saucepan	1 min	Hot
11. Mix in a bowl	2 tabls 1 tabls 1 teasp 1 teasp	Milk Cornflour Tomato Puree Sugar	Strain milk from fish into this. Pour the mixture into the butter, stir constantly with a wooden spoon and boil	2 min	Hot
12. Sieve the onions and wine into this mixture			Stir well in for	½ min	Hot
13. Stir in	1 tabls	Sherry			
14. Season with		Salt, Pepper			
15. Stir in	2oz/56g	Frozen Shrimps	Add any liquid from the warm fish, mix well in. Pour sauce over fish		
16. Chop finely	3 teasp	Parsley	Sprinkle over the pink sauce and serve		

Fisherman's Pie

Overall time:
1¼ hr

Process	Amount	Ingredients	Explanation	Time	Heat
1. Bring to the boil	2pt/1¼lt	Water	In a saucepan		Hot
2. Peel and slice	2 large	Potatoes	Add to the water. Cook	20 min	Med
3. Meanwhile, put	12oz/337g	Fish (white fillets)	In a saucepan		
4. Pour over	½pt/280ml	Milk	Bring to the boil	2 min	Hot
5. Sprinkle over		Salt, Pepper			
6. Add	1	Bayleaf	Cover pan and cook	10 min	Low
7. Meanwhile, chop very finely	1 medium	Onion			
8. Melt in a saucepan	1oz/28g	Butter	Using a wooden spoon	1 min	Hot
9. Add the onions			Fry and stir till soft and golden	8 min	Med
10. Sprinkle and stir	2 tabls	Plain Flour	Into the onions		V.Low
11. Pour over	¼pt/140ml	Milk	Stir well in		
12. Transfer the fish to a plate			Strain the milk into the onions		
13. Season with		Salt, Pepper	Cook, stirring constantly Take off heat. Cover pan	3 min	Med
14. Skin and bone fish			Flake it and put it in an ovenproof dish		
15. Pour the sauce			Over the fish		
16. Chop and add	3 teasp	Parsley	Stir mixture carefully together		
17. Drain the potatoes			Mash with a potato masher or fork		
18. Beat in	1oz/28g	Butter	With a wooden spoon		
19. Beat in	4 tabls	Milk			
20. Grate and mix in	2oz/56g	Cheese	Spread on top of the fish in sauce with a fork		
21. Grate on top	2oz/56g	Cheese	Cook in oven till brown	20 min	Hot

49 Squid Stewed with Spicy Paprika and Wine Sauce

Overall time: 2¼ hr

I serve this with rice or with plain boiled white beans (these need two hours to boil, though), or with crispy, white french bread to dip in the sauce.

Process	Amount	Ingredients	Explanation	Time	Heat
1. Clean and cut	12oz/337g	Squid	In bite-size bits		
2. Heat in a saucepan	1 tabls	Oil	Add the squid and cook	10 min	Low
3. Meanwhile, trim and chop	4	Spring Onions	Add to the squid		
4. De-seed and chop	½	Red Pepper	Add to the squid and cook	5 min	Low
5. Add and mix well	½ tabls	Tomato Puree			
6. Season with	½ teasp	Salt, Pepper Garlic (powder or fresh)			
	¼ teasp	Cayenne	(More if you like it hot)		
	2 teasp	Paprika			
7. Chop and add	1 tabls	Parsley	Mix well together		
8. Chop and add	1 tabls	Fennel (if available)	Mix well in		
9. Stir in	¼pt/140ml	Wine			
10. Stir in	¼pt/140ml	Water			
11. Stir in	1 teasp	Vinegar	Cover pan and cook	1½ hr	V. Low

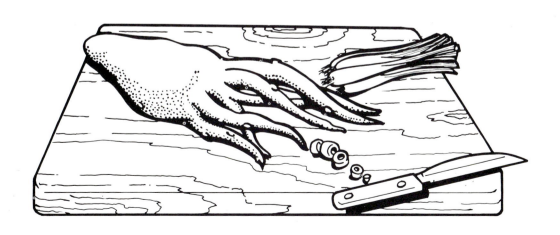

Greek Beef and Egg Roll

An appetizing way of using the cheapest of all meats. It is good cold but best hot. You can serve it in slices with tomato sauce (see 97) and rice, or potatoes baked in their skins, and any green vegetable.

Process	Amount	Ingredients	Explanation	Time	Heat
1. Boil	2	Eggs	In a saucepan of water	10 min	Hot
2. Meanwhile, beat	1	Egg	In a bowl	2 min	
3. Crumble in	2 slices	Bread	Mix with beaten egg		
4. Season with	½ teasp	Salt, Pepper Cinnamon			
5. Add and mix well	12oz/337g	Minced Beef	Preheat the oven		Med
6. Chop and add	1 teasp	Mint			
7. Melt and add	1oz/28g	Butter	Mix very thoroughly		
8. Spread this mixture			Flat on a baking tray		
9. Shell cooked eggs			Put them in the centre of the meat. Mould meat up round them into a roll with the eggs in the centre. Cover in foil		
10. Place on baking tray			Cook in the oven	35 min	Med

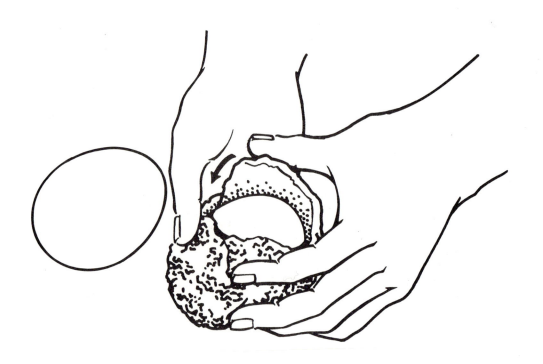

51 Hamburgers and Tomato and Basil Sauce with Rice

Overall time:
45 min

Process	Amount	Ingredients	Explanation	Time	Heat
1. Peel and chop fine	1 medium	Onion			
2. Melt in a saucepan	1oz/28g	Butter	Add onions. Stir with a wooden spoon	8 min	Med
3. Chop fine and add	8oz/225g	Tomatoes (1 small tin)	Stir well together		
4. Season with	2 teasp ½ teasp	Salt, Pepper Basil Tabasco			
5. Mix well in	1 teasp	Sugar	Cover pan and cook	20 min	Low
6. Meanwhile, bring to the boil	½pt/280ml	Water	In another saucepan	2 min	Hot
7. Add	½ teasp	Salt			
8. Stir in	4oz/112g	Rice	Cover pan and cook Take off heat and leave covered for	10 min 5 min	Med
9. Meanwhile, put	12oz/337g	Lean Minced Beef	In a bowl		
10. Add		Salt, Pepper	With your hands, firmly turn, press and mix the mince and seasoning till it is a compact roll. Cut it in half and mould the halves into round balls. Flatten them firmly with the palm of your hand.		
11. Heat very well	1 tabls	Oil	In a frying pan. Cook hamburgers for on either side	2 min	Hot
12. Serve hamburgers surrounded by the rice and sauce					

52 Steak in a Piquant Cream Sauce

The best steak to use is rump or entrecôte. One of my favourites for speed and flavour.

Overall time:
20 min

Process	Amount	Ingredients	Explanation	Time	Heat
1. Pour into a bowl	¼pt/140ml	Cream			
2. Season with	1 teasp	Salt, Pepper Worcestershire Sauce			
	1 teasp	Mustard	Mix well		
3. Melt	2oz/56g	Butter	In a frying pan	1 min	Hot
4. Add and fry	2 7oz/196g	Frying Steaks	Brown one side well	4 min	Med
			Turn. Fry other side	4 min	Med
5. Remove meat from pan			Keep warm in oven		V.Low
6. Pour cream mixture			Over juices in pan		Low
7. Stir together			With a wooden spoon scraping sediment from base of pan and mixing all together	2 min	Med
8. Pour this sauce			Over the meat		
9. Chop finely	1 teasp	Parsley	Sprinkle over and serve		

Steak and Kidney Casserole

Easier than pie, and certainly less fattening. You don't have to pre-cook anything; just prepare, mix and pop in the oven. Good with potatoes in their jackets and cabbage, broccoli or sprouts.

Overall time:
2½ hr

Process	Amount	Ingredients	Explanation	Time	Heat
1. Trim and cut	8oz/225g	Stewing Steak	Into bite-size bits		
2. Trim and cut	6oz/169g	Kidneys (Lambs' or Calves')	Into bite-size bits. Mix these together in an ovenproof dish		
3. Sprinkle over	1 tabls ½ teasp	Salt, Pepper Flour Mixed Herbs	Mix very thoroughly, so that all the meat bits are floured		
4. Peel and cut small	1 large	Onion	Add to meat and mix		
5. Clean and cut small	2 medium	Carrots	Add to meat and mix		
6. Pour over	½pt/280ml	Water	Stir well together. Cover dish and cook in the oven slowly for Stir from time to time and if it gets too dry add a few tablespoons more water	2 hrs	Med
7. Chop finely	1 tabls	Parsley	Stir in half and sprinkle the rest on top		

Lamb Cutlet Joint Roast
with Bacon and Mushroom

Overall time:
1½ hr

Ask for Best End (i.e. Rack) of Lamb. If you want a simpler roast, just leave out the onions, mushrooms and bacon.

Process	Amount	Ingredients	Explanation	Time	Heat
1. Peel and chop	1 small	Onion			
2. Melt in a saucepan	½oz/14g	Butter	Add onions and stir Cover pan. Lower heat	3 min	Med V.Low
3. Clean and chop small	2oz/56g	Mushrooms	Add to onions. Stir for	5 mins	Med
4. Chop finely	2 teasp	Parsley	Add and stir well		V.Low
5. Season with		Salt, Pepper			
6. Trim	4 or 6	Lamb Cutlets in a piece	Put the piece in a frying pan skin-side down till skin is golden	Approx 3 min	Hot
7. Transfer the meat			To a roasting oven-tin		
8. Sprinkle		Pepper and Salt	All over the meat		
9. Sprinkle	½ teasp	Garlic (powder or fresh)	Over the bone side of the meat		
10. With a sharp knife			Make little cuts between each bone at the thick end		
11. Chop small and rub	½ teasp	Rosemary	Into the cuts. Spread the mushroom mixture over and into the cuts		
12. De-rind	4 slices	Bacon	Wrap them over the mushroom mixture		
13. Secure the bacon with		Toothpicks	Stuck into meat		
14. Lay the meat bacon-side down in roasting tin			Cook in oven	40 min	Med
15. Transfer meat to a serving dish			Pour away fat in roasting tin		
16. Add	4 tabls	Water	To the juices from meat Bring to boil, stirring	1 min	Hot
17. Carve joint			Serve gravy mixture in a gravy boat		

55 Lamb with Courgettes

**Overall time:
2 hr**

This can be served with rice, noodles, or potatoes either boiled or baked in their jackets. Get the butcher to bone and chop the lamb for you if you can. Make sure it is well seasoned with salt and pepper at the end.

Process	Amount	Ingredients	Explanation	Time	Heat
1. Bone and cube	1lb/450g	Lamb (shoulder or leg)	In bite-size bits, removing the fat		
2. Peel and chop finely	1 large	Onion			
3. Melt	1oz/28g	Butter	In a saucepan		
4. Add the onions and meat			Fry and stir for	10 min	Med
5. Chop small	1lb/450g	Tomatoes (1 medium tin)	Add to meat and onions		Med
6. Season with		Salt, Pepper			
	2 teasp	Sugar			
Chop finely and add	3 teasp	Mint			
Chop finely and add	2 teasp	Parsley	Mix all well together		Med
7. Chop finely and add	1 large or	Garlic Clove			
	1 teasp	Garlic Powder	Stir well. Cover and cook	45 min	Low
8. Heat	1 tabls	Oil	In a frying pan		V.Low
9. Clean, slice and add	4 medium	Courgettes	Fry and stir	5 min	Hot
10. Add to lamb stew			Check seasoning. Cover again and continue cooking gently for	30 min	Low

Lamb and Potatoes Baked with Tomato and Rosemary

Overall time:
1¾ hr

A hearty, tasty meal, very good with any kind of green beans.

Process	Amount	Ingredients	Explanation	Time	Heat
1. Peel and chop	1 medium	Onion			
2. Heat	1 tabls	Oil	In a frying pan	1 min	Hot
3. Add	1 thick slice	Leg of Lamb	Fry each side for until golden brown	Approx 4 min	Hot
4. Transfer meat			To an ovenproof dish		
5. Add onions to oil			Cook, stirring constantly with a wooden spoon for about scraping the sediment up from the base of the pan	5 min	Med
6. Add and stir well	½pt/280ml	Water	Bring to the boil	2 min	Hot
7. Mix in	1 tabls	Tomato Puree			
8. Season with	1 teasp 1 teasp	Salt, Pepper Sugar Garlic (fresh or dried)	Stir well together		Med
9. Mix in	1 teasp	Rosemary	Pour this sauce under the meat in the ovenproof dish		
10. Peel and slice	2 large	Potatoes	Arrange round meat. Cover and cook in oven	1 hr	Med
11. Remove cover			Cook for a further till meat is browned	15 min	Med

Lamb Chops delicately flavoured with Orange, Lemon and Garlic

**Overall time:
30 min**

An excellent way to make chops taste deliciously different.

Process	Amount	Ingredients	Explanation	Time	Heat
1. Preheat oven					Hot
2. Melt	1oz/28g	Butter	In a frying pan	1 min	Hot
3. Add	2 large	Lamb Chops (shoulder or chump)	Fry on each side for until golden brown	4 min	Hot
4. Sprinkle on each one		Salt Lemon Pepper (or grated Lemon Peel) Garlic Powder	Transfer meat to an ovenproof dish		
5. Add to pan	6 tabls	Water	Boil and stir with a wooden spoon, scraping the sediment from the base of the pan for	1 min	Hot
6. Add and stir well	2 tabls	Orange Juice	Pour over the chops Cover and cook in oven	15 min	Hot
7. Chop finely	2 teasp	Parsley	Sprinkle over and serve		

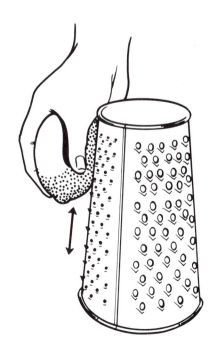

Pork Fillet with a Three-Fruit Sauce lightly flavoured with Curry

Overall time:
1 hr

You can use any three fruits. Serve it with boiled rice or potatoes, green beans, peas, or broccoli. If you can find mange-tout they are lovely with it.

Process	Amount	Ingredients	Explanation	Time	Heat
1. Melt	2oz/56g	Butter	In a frying pan	1 min	Hot
2. Cut in six slices	1 whole	Pork Fillet	Cook each side for until golden brown. Put in ovenproof dish	3 min	Hot
3. Add to frying pan	2 teasp	Curry Powder	Stir with a wooden spoon	1 min	Low
4. Add and stir well	1 tabls	Flour			
5. Add and stir well	¼pt/140ml	Milk	Scraping sediment from the base of the pan		
6. Add and stir well	½	Chicken cube	Until dissolved		
7. Season with		Salt, Pepper	Bring to the boil	1 min	Hot
8. Add and stir well	2 tabls	Sherry	Cook, stirring constantly Cover pan and leave	3 min	Low
9. Cut in thin slices	½ ½ ½	Apple Orange Peach (or any mixture of any three fruits)	Put them on top of the meat in the ovenproof dish. Pour the sauce over the top. Cover and put in oven	30 min	Med
10. Transfer the meat to a serving dish			Reheat sauce	2 min	Hot
11. Sieve the fruit			Stir it with the sauce, and pour over the meat		
12. Peel and slice	1	Kiwi Fruit (optional)	Arrange around the meat		
13. Chop finely	2 teasp	Parsley	Sprinkle on top and serve		

Pork Chops with Apples and Cider

This is best accompanied by broad beans and/or glazed carrots and peas (see 83) and potatoes, sliced thin and cooked in the oven with butter (see 90).

Overall time:
1 hr

Process	Amount	Ingredients	Explanation	Time	Heat
1. Melt	1oz/28g	Butter	In a frying pan	1 min	Hot
2. Fry till golden	2	Pork Chops	Cook each side about Cover pan. Lower heat Preheat oven	4 min	Hot Low Med
3. Peel and chop	2 medium	Onions			
4. Melt in a saucepan	½oz/14g	Butter	Add onions. Cook and stir	5 min	Med
5. Peel and slice	1	Apple	Into the onions and stir	3 mins	Med
6. Sprinkle on	1 teasp	Flour	Stir well together		Low
7. Add and stir	¼pt/140ml	Cider (or Water)			
8. Stir in	½	Chicken cube	Until dissolved		
9. Season with		Salt, Pepper	Stir in		
10. Transfer the meat to an ovenproof dish					
11. Pour the sauce into the frying pan			Mix with the juices. Scrape all the sediment from the base of the pan with a wooden spoon and mix in		
12. Bring to the boil			Cook, stirring constantly	2 min	Med
13. Pour this mixture over the meat			Cook in the oven for	30 min	Med
14. Chop finely	2 teasp	Parsley	Sprinkle over and serve		

60 Pork Pieces with Lychee Sauce

**Overall time:
45 min**

This can be made with belly of pork or spare rib chops or any piece of boneless pork. The sweet-sour Chinese-type sauce is extra-exotic with the lychees. It's very good with plain boiled rice and Spring Onion Crisps (see 81) or broccoli.

Process	Amount	Ingredients	Explanation	Time	Heat
1. Put in a bowl	1 tabls	Sherry	Preheat the oven		Med
2. Add and stir	1 tabls	Soya Sauce			
3. Add and stir	½ teasp	Salt			
4. Trim fat off and cube in bite-size bits	12oz	Pork Pieces	Mix well with the sherry mixture in the bowl till cubes are well-coated		
5. Put cubes in an ovenproof dish			Put in the oven to dry for	10 min	Med
6. Melt in a frying pan	1oz/28g	Butter	Add cubes. Cook and stir	15 min	Med
7. Put in a small bowl	2 tabls	Cold Water			
8. Add and stir well	1 tabls	Cornflour			
9. Add and stir well	1 tabls	Tomato Puree			
10. Add	1 tabls	Vinegar			
11. Add	1 tabls	Sherry			
12. Add and stir well in	1 tabls	Sugar	Mix all well together		
13. Add the juice from	1 small tin (approx 6oz/168g)	Lychees	Pour this mixture over the pork and boil, stirring constantly with a wooden spoon and scraping all the sediment from the pan for	5 min	Med
14. Put in a serving dish			Surround the pork with the lychees		
15. Chop finely	2 teasp	Chives or Spring Onion tops	Sprinkle over and serve		

Pork (or Beef) Stewed with Paprika and Potatoes

Overall time:
2¼ hr

My version of Goulash. Wonderfully tasty, easy to prepare, inexpensive (if you use beef, just get cubed stewing steak). Good for reheating, or keeping warm for buffets. Serve it with green beans, broccoli or cabbage.

Process	Amount	Ingredients	Explanation	Time	Heat
1. Trim and cut	12oz/337g	Pork Belly or Boneless Spare Rib Steaks	Into bite-size pieces		
2. Melt in a frying pan	1oz/28g	Butter	Add meat. Stir and fry Transfer meat to ovenproof dish	5 min	Hot
3. Peel and chop	1 large	Onion	Cook in frying pan for stirring constantly	5 min	Med
4. Sprinkle on and stir	2 teasp	Flour			
5. Chop small and add	½lb/225g	Tomatoes (1 small tin)	Stir well together		
6. De-seed and chop	1 medium	Red Pepper	Add to the tomatoes		
7. Clean and chop small	2 medium	Carrots	Add to the tomatoes		
8. Season with	1 tabls 1 teasp 1 teasp	Salt, Pepper Paprika Sugar Garlic (powder or fresh)	Mix well together		
9. Add and stir well	1 tabls	Vinegar	Pour this mixture over the meat and stir well. Cover the ovenproof dish. Cook in oven	1 hr	Med
10. Meanwhile, peel and quarter	2 medium	Potatoes	Boil in a pan of salted water for	15 min	Med
11. Drain potatoes. Add to the stew If stew is dry, add	3 or 4 tabls	Water	Stir well in. Cover dish. Cook in oven	30 min	Med

62   Veal and Green Bean Ragout

I learned about this dish in Greece, and serve it with rice, or potatoes baked in their skins.

**Overall time:
2 hr**

Process	Amount	Ingredients	Explanation	Time	Heat
1. Melt	2oz/56g	Butter	In a frying pan	1 min	Hot
2. Fry and stir	12oz/337g	Stewing Veal (cubed)	Till golden brown Lower heat	approx 5 min	Hot Low
3. Peel and chop small	1 large	Onion	Transfer the meat to a saucepan, add onions to frying pan. Cook and stir with a wooden spoon, scraping sediment from base of pan and mixing well	5 min	Med
4. Sprinkle on	2 teasp	Flour			
5. Stir in	¼pt/140ml	Water	Mix well together		Low
6. Stir in Season with	 2 tabls 1 piece 2 1 teasp 1 teasp	Salt, Pepper Vinegar Lemon Rind Bayleaves Garlic Marjoram			
7. Stir in	1 teasp	Sugar	Pour this mixture over the meat		
8. Peel and chop small	8oz/225g	Tomatoes (1 small tin)	Add to the meat and mix well. Boil	3 min	Hot
9. Cover the pan			Allow to cook gently	1½ hr	Low
10. Prepare	8oz/225g	Green Beans	Cook till tender in boiling salted water. Add them to the stew during the last half-hour	5 min	Med
11. Chop finely	3 teasp	Parsley	Stir in		

63 Fricassée of Veal or Pork

**Overall time:
1 hr**

My mother's version of this famous dish. You can use leftover chicken or turkey equally well — just omit stage 4.

Process	Amount	Ingredients	Explanation	Time	Heat
1. Cut	12oz/337g	Veal or Pork Escallops	In bite-size bits		
2. Chop finely	1 large	Onion	Preheat oven		Med
3. Melt	2oz/56g	Butter	In a frying pan	1 min	Hot
4. Add, fry and stir			The meat till brown	5 min	Med
5. Transfer the meat			To an ovenproof dish		
6. Add the onions to frying pan			Fry and stir till golden	5 min	Med
7. Chop and stir in	2oz/56g	Mushrooms	With a wooden spoon, scraping sediment from the base of the pan	3 min	Med
8. Sprinkle on and stir	2 tabls	Flour	Mix well together		Low
9. Add and stir well	½pt/280ml	Milk	Bring to the boil stirring constantly	2 min	Hot
10. Season with		Salt, Pepper			
11. Add	2 tabls	Vermouth (optional)	Pour over the meat and mix well together		
12. Grate over the top	2oz/56g	Cheese	Cook in the oven for till golden brown	30 min	Med
13. Chop finely	2 teasp	Parsley	Sprinkle over and serve		

Sliced Shin of Veal on the Bone with Wine, Lemon and Vegetables

My version of the famous Italian dish *osso bucco*. Serve it with rice and a green vegetable. (You can cook any stewing veal or shoulder of veal in this mouthwatering way but the marrow in the piece of bone is special.)

Process	Amount	Ingredients	Explanation	Time	Heat
1. Melt in a frying pan	2oz/56g	Butter	Using a wooden spoon	1 min	Hot
2. Fry till golden brown	2 slices	Veal Shin on the Bone 1"/2½cm Thick	Giving each side about	4 min	Med
3. Transfer veal to an ovenproof dish					
4. De-rind and cut in bite-size bits	4 slices	Bacon	Fry in same butter for about	3 min	Med
5. Add bacon to veal			Pour the butter into a saucepan		
6. Pour into frying pan	½pt/280ml	Water			
7. Add and stir well	6 tabls	Wine	Scrape the sediment from the base of the pan with a wooden spoon		Low
8. Stir in and dissolve	½	Chicken cube	Boil, stirring constantly for Take off heat, cover pan, and keep	2 min	Hot
9. Peel and chop finely	1 large	Onion	Fry in saucepan with butter	5 min	Med
10. Clean, chop and add	2 medium	Carrots	Mix well with onions		Med
11. De-string, chop and add	2 sticks	Celery	Mix all together in pan	3 min	Med
12. Sprinkle over	1 tabls	Flour	Stir well		
13. Season with		Salt, Pepper	Add vegetables to the wine mixture in the frying pan. Stir well		
14. Add	1	Bayleaf	Bring to boil and stir	3 min	Med
15. Chop finely and add	2 tabls	Parsley	Mix well together		
16. Grate on top the rind of	1	Lemon	Mix well	1 min	Med
17. Pour this mixture over veal and bacon			Cover ovenproof dish and cook in the oven for	1½ hr	Med
18. Chop finely	2 teasp	Parsley	Sprinkle over and serve		

Hot Ham in Wine Sauce with Spinach Puree

**Overall time:
40 mins**

I think mashed potatoes are best with this. You can serve peas or broccoli or beans instead of the spinach.

Process	Amount	Ingredients	Explanation	Time	Heat
1. Melt	1oz/28g	Butter	In a frying pan	1 min	Hot
2. Add	4 thick slices	Cooked Ham	Fry both sides for about till golden. Cover pan	2 min	Med V.Low
3. Put	3 teasp	Bisto	In a small bowl		
4. Add	¼pt/140ml	Wine	Mix very well		
5. Add	4 tabls	Cold Water	Mix very well		
6. Season with	2 teasp 2 teasp	Salt, Pepper English Mustard Sugar	Mix well together		
7. Pour this mixture over the ham Lower heat			Boil and stir for about Cover pan and cook	1 min 10 min	Hot V.Low
8. Bring to the boil Add	¼pt/140ml ½ teasp	Water Salt	In a saucepan	2 min	Hot
9. Wash well and add	8oz/225g	Spinach (or Frozen Spinach)	Boil till tender. About Drain well and chop very finely	8 min	Med
10. Melt Season with	1oz/28g	Butter Salt, Pepper	In a saucepan Add spinach and mix well	1 min	Hot Low
11. Put	2 teasp	Cornflour	In a small bowl		
12. Add	¼pt/140ml	Milk	Mix in very well		
13. Add and stir in	¼ teasp	Sugar	Pour over the spinach		
14. Bring to the boil			Stir constantly with a wooden spoon	3 min	Hot
15. Serve the ham			Topped by the wine sauce and surrounded with the spinach		

66 Kidneys with a Devilled Wine Sauce and Juniper Berries

Overall time:
30 min

If you can't get juniper berries, don't despair — the kidneys are excellent, even without them. Serve surrounded with peas or green beans.

Process	Amount	Ingredients	Explanation	Time	Heat
1. Bring to the boil	½pt/280ml	Water	In a saucepan	2 min	Hot
2. Add and stir well	4oz/112g	Rice	Cover pan and cook for	12 min	Low
3. Meanwhile, trim	4	Lambs' Kidneys (6 if small)	Cut into bite size pieces		
4. Melt in a frying pan	2oz/56g	Butter	Add kidneys, stir and cook	5 min	Med
5. Cover the frying pan			Cook gently	3 min	Low
6. Meanwhile, put Add	2 teasp 4 tabls 1 teasp 1 teasp 2 teasp 2 teasp	Salt, Pepper Bisto Wine English Mustard Sugar Lea & Perrins Lemon Juice	Into a small bowl Stir well. Pour this mixture over the kidneys and stir well.		
7. Crush and cut small	8	Juniper Berries (if available)	Add and stir well. Cover pan and cook for	10 min	Low
8. Take rice off heat			Leave with the lid on till needed		
9. Chop finely	2 teasp	Parsley	Serve the kidneys on a bed of rice sprinkled with the parsley		

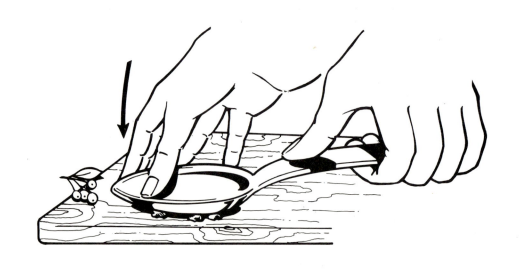

Rabbit with Bacon and Onion Sauce

You can use chicken for this, but the rabbit gives it a special flavour. Serve with plain boiled potatoes (baby new ones, if possible) and beans, peas or courgettes.

Overall time:
45 min

Process	Amount	Ingredients	Explanation	Time	Heat
1. Peel and chop	1 large	Onion			
2. Melt in a frying pan	1oz/28g	Butter	Using a wooden spoon for	1 min	Hot
3. Add and cook	4 slices	Bacon	Till brown. About	3 min	Med
4. Transfer bacon to a plate			Add onions to fat in frying pan. Stir well Cover pan and cook	1 min 5 min	Med Low
5. De-rind the bacon			Cut in bite-size bits		
6. Trim and cut or Use	1lb/450g ¾lb/337g	Rabbit Cubed Rabbit Meat	In bite-size bits Add to onions in pan. Cook, stirring constantly till golden, scraping up the sediment from the base of the pan with a wooden spoon	5 min	Low
7. Sprinkle over	2 teasp	Flour	Stir well		
8. Season with	 2 teasp	Salt, Pepper Tarragon	Add bacon bits Mix well in		
9. Pour on	½pt/280g	Milk	Boil, stirring constantly	2 min	Hot
10. Add and stir in	2	Bayleaves	Lower heat. Cover pan and cook till tender	Approx 20 min	Low
11. Add	2/3 tabls	Milk (optional)	Stir well together	½ min	
12. Chop finely	2 teasp	Parsley	Sprinkle over and serve		

Hot Ox Tongue with Mustard and Parsley Sauce

Overall time:
2½ hrs

The tongue is served sliced surrounded with boiled new potatoes, or with mashed potatoes, and sprinkled with parsley; the sauce served separately. Lightly boiled buttered cabbage is particularly good with it, or spring greens or spinach.

Process	Amount	Ingredients	Explanation	Time	Heat
1. Put in a big saucepan	1 small	Ox Tongue	Cover with cold water		
2. Add	6	Peppercorns	Bring to the boil		Hot
3. Lower heat and add (If the tongue is unsalted, add	3 4 teasp	Bayleaves Salt)	Cover pan and cook for about or until it feels tender when you stick a fork in	2 hrs	Low
4. Take the tongue from the water			Run cold water over it till cool		
5. Remove the skin			Replace tongue in the hot water it was boiled in		V.Low
6. Melt in a saucepan	2oz/56g	Butter	Using a wooden spoon	1 min	Med
7. Add and stir well	2 tabls	Flour	Remove from heat		
8. Add, stir and boil	½pt/280ml	Milk	Beat with an eggbeater	2 min	Hot
9. Add and mix well	3 teasp	English Mustard	Take off heat		
10. Season with	 2 teasp 1 tabls	Salt, Pepper Sugar Vinegar	 Beat with an eggbeater	 1 min	
11. Chop finely and add	1 tabls	Parsley	Return to heat. Stir for	2 min	Med
12. Drain and slice thin			Required amount of ox tongue. Lay on a dish		

For the remaining piece of tongue

13. Put remaining piece into a bowl			Add 4/5 spoons of the liquid it was boiled in		
14. Cover with a plate small enough to press down on the tongue					
15. Put something heavy on the plate			Leave overnight		
16. Serve sliced cold			With jacket potatoes and salad		

69 Chicken Breasts Stuffed with Ham and Gruyère with a Vermouth Sauce

Overall time:
1 hr

Especially good with asparagus, but broccoli or beans and celery or peas and new or boiled potatoes are excellent.

Process	Amount	Ingredients	Explanation	Time	Heat
1. Melt	1oz/28g	Butter	In a frying pan	½ min	Hot
2. Add and fry	2 each about 7oz/186g	Chicken Breasts off the bone	On each side for about till golden brown	3 min	Med
3. Turn off heat			Put chicken in an oven-proof dish (keep frying pan with butter). Make a deep sideways incision in each breast		
4. Into each split, put	1 teasp	Butter			
5. Lightly sprinkle		Garlic Powder	Into each of the slits		
6. Into the slits, push	2 slices	Ham	One slice per breast		
7. Into the slits, push	2 slices	Gruyère	One slice per breast		
8. Sprinkle with		Lemon Pepper, Salt	Put in the oven		Med
9. Sprinkle and stir	2 teasp	Flour	Into the butter that the chicken was fried in		
10. Crumble over	½	Chicken cube			
11. Add, boil and stir	½pt/280ml	Milk	With a wooden spoon, for scraping in all the sediment from base of pan	2 min	Hot
12. Take off heat. Add	2 tabls	Vermouth	Stir well into sauce		
13. Season with		Salt, Pepper	Pour sauce *around* the chicken, not on top		
14. Return to oven			Cook in oven for	25 min	Med
15. Chop finely	2 teasp	Parsley	Sprinkle over and serve		

Chicken with Cucumber

Overall time:
45 min

This is equally good with either breast or leg. (If you use legs, cut them in half lengthwise and allow 10 mins extra at stage 5 in the oven). Serve with new or mashed potatoes and french beans or petits pois and glazed carrots (see 83).

Process	Amount	Ingredients	Explanation	Time	Heat
1. Melt	1oz/28g	Butter	In a frying pan	½ min	Hot
2. Fry until golden	2 each about 7oz/196g	Chicken Pieces	Cook each side about Cover pan for	3 min 5 min	Med V.Low
3. Peel and cut	6"/15cm	Cucumber	Into 6 pieces and then into 6 cubes per piece		
4. Add cucumber to pan with chicken			Cover pan and cook	10 min	Low
5. Take pan off heat. Add		Salt, Pepper	Put chicken in an ovenproof dish in the oven	10 min	Med
6. Meanwhile, add to cucumber in pan	1 tabls	Flour	Stir well		
7. Heat	4 tabls	Water	In a small saucepan	1 min	Hot
8. Add and dissolve	½	Chicken cube			
9. Add and stir well	¼pt/140ml	Milk	Pour this mixture over the cucumber mixture		
10. Return to heat. Add		Salt, Pepper	Stir constantly for Reduce heat and cook for	1 min 2 min	Hot V.Low
11. Pour this sauce over the chicken			Cook in the oven for	10 min	Med
12. Chop finely	2 teasp	Parsley	Sprinkle over and serve		

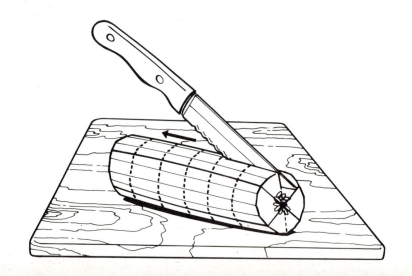

Chicken Breasts with a Duxelles Mushroom Stuffing and Whisky Sauce

Overall time:
1 hr

Very good with rosti potatoes (89), or Anna Potatoes (90).

Process	Amount	Ingredients	Explanation	Time	Heat
1. Peel and chop	1 medium	Onion	Very, very finely		
2. Melt in a saucepan	1oz/28g	Butter	Add the onions and cook, stirring constantly	5 min	Med
Add and stir in	1 teasp	Tarragon	Lower heat. Cover pan, allow to cook		V.Low
3. Chop	4oz/112g	Mushrooms	In tiny pieces. Add to the onions. Cook, stirring occasionally, for	5 min	Med
4. Add and stir well		Salt, Pepper			
5. Chop very finely	3 teasp	Parsley	Mix well in. Take off heat		
6. Remove bones from	2	Chicken Breasts			
7. Melt in a frying pan	1oz/28g	Butter	Add chicken and cook each side till golden for	5 min	Med
8. Transfer chicken to an ovenproof dish			Preheat oven		Hot
9. Sprinkle into saucepan	1 teasp	Flour	Stir well off the heat with a wooden spoon scraping all the sediment from the base of the pan		
Stir in	6 tabls	Water			
Season with		Salt, Pepper			
10. Return pan to heat			Bring to the boil and stir constantly for	2 min	Hot
11. Add and stir well in	2 tabls	Whisky	Take off heat. Cover pan		
12. Cut a deep slit in the side of each chicken piece so that they are like pockets					
13. Sprinkle		Garlic Powder	Inside and fill them with the mushroom mixture		
14. Sprinkle well with		Lemon Pepper	Pour the whisky mixture over the chicken and cook in the oven for	15 min	Hot

Chicken Breasts with Cider and Pink Shrimp Sauce

Overall time:
50 min

Serve this with baby new potatoes or puree potatoes, and petits pois with chopped roasted almonds or green beans with finely chopped green pepper.

Process	Amount	Ingredients	Explanation	Time	Heat
1. Chop very finely	1 small	Onion	Put in a saucepan		
2. Pour in Season with	6 tabls 1	Cider Salt, Pepper Bayleaf			
3. Put on top	2 each about 7oz/196g	Chicken Breasts	Bring to the boil Lower heat. Cover pan for	2 min 30 min	Hot Low
4. Transfer chicken to a serving dish			Discard skin and bones, cover and keep warm in the oven.		V.Low
5. Discard bayleaf			Sieve or liquidize the cider and onion		
6. Melt in a saucepan	2oz/56g	Butter	Using a wooden spoon	1 min	Hot
7. Add and stir	1 tabls	Flour	Take off heat		
8. Add and stir well	4 tabls	Milk	Add the sieved sauce, return to the heat		Hot
9. Season with Stir in	 1 teasp	Salt, Pepper Tomato Puree	Beat with an eggbeater	3 min	Med
10. Add	2oz/56g	Shelled Prawns (fresh or frozen)	Stir well with a wooden spoon	2 min	Low
11. Chop finely	2 teasp	Parsley	Pour the sauce over the chicken breasts. Sprinkle with parsley and serve		

Chicken with Wine and Tiny Onions and Bacon

Overall time:
1 hr

A quick and easy coq-au-vin. It is equally good in large amounts for a buffet party and perfect if the party is after-cinema or theatre as you can happily reheat it.

Process	Amount	Ingredients	Explanation	Time	Heat
1. Melt in a frying pan	½oz/14g	Butter	Using a wooden spoon	½ min	Hot
2. Add and fry	2 pieces	Chicken (breast or leg)	On each side, for about till golden brown	3 min	Med
3. Transfer chicken to a saucepan			Keep frying pan with fat in it		
4. Pour over the chicken	½pt/280ml	Wine			
5. Season with Add and dissolve	½ 2 teasp	Salt, Pepper Chicken cube Sugar	Bring to the boil	2 min	Hot
6. Stir in	2 teasp	Mixed Herbs	Cover pan. Lower heat		Low
7. Fry	4 slices	Bacon	In the same frying pan Take off heat. Remove bacon	3 min	Med
8. Peel and add Peel and chop	20 tiny or 1 medium	Onions Onion	Fry and stir till golden in the same frying pan	5 min	Med
9. Remove pan from heat			De-rind bacon. Cut in bite-size bits		
10. Add onions and bacon to the chicken					
11. Sprinkle into the fat in the frying pan	1 teasp	Flour	Stir well		
12. Pour in	¼pt/140ml	Water	Stir very well, scraping the sediment from the base of the pan. Boil	2 min	Med
13. Pour this sauce over the chicken			Stir well in. Cover pan. Cook	30 min	Low
14. Chop finely	2 teasp	Parsley	Sprinkle over and serve		

Poached Chicken with Tuna Fish Sauce

**Overall Time:
2 hrs**

A cold dinner, lunch or buffet dish, excellent served with cold new potatoes or potato salad and beetroot, but any salad will go well. (This dish is usually done with a piece of well-boiled veal. The Italian Vitello Tonnato.)

Process	Amount	Ingredients	Explanation	Time	Heat
1. Peel and chop roughly	1 medium	Onion	Put in a saucepan		
2. Scrape and chop roughly	1 medium	Carrot	Put in the saucepan		
3. Wash, de-string and chop	2 sticks	Celery	Add to saucepan		
4. Crumble in	1	Chicken cube			
5. Stir in	¾pt/420ml	Water	Cover pan and cook	25 min	Med
6. Put in and immerse	2	Chicken Breasts	Cover pan and cook	10 min	Hot
7. Turn off heat			Leave in pan till cold		
8. Sieve or liquidize the vegetables and stock			Discard skin and bones		
9. Slice the chicken Sprinkle thinly with	¼ teasp	Salt Lemon Pepper	Arrange the slices overlapping on a serving dish		
10. Boil vegetable puree			Till there are approx 6 tabls of it left	3-5 min	Hot
11. Mash thoroughly or liquidize	3½oz/100g	Tuna Fish (1 small tin)	Add to the vegetable puree		
12. Allow to cool and add	4 tabls	Mayonnaise	Mix well together		
13. Season with	a few drops 1 teasp	Pepper Tabasco Anchovy Essence (optional)	Mix well together and pour over the chicken		
14. Sprinkle over	1 tabls	Capers	Cover the dish and keep cold till needed		
15. Decorate with		Watercress (optional)	Serve		

Poached Chicken with Orange and Lemon Sauce

Overall time:
1¼ hr

Serve with baby new potatoes or half jacket potatoes (see p.xviii) and any green vegetable.

Process	Amount	Ingredients	Explanation	Time	Heat
1. Put in a saucepan	1 small	Chicken	Cover with water Bring to the boil		Hot
2. Crumble in	1	Chicken cube	Cover pan and boil	10 min	Hot
3. Turn off heat. Stir in	½ teasp	Salt	Leave chicken in covered pan of water for at least	30 min	
4. Meanwhile, peel and chop finely	1 medium	Onion			
5. Melt in a saucepan	1oz/28g	Butter	Add onions. Cook and stir	5 min	Med
6. Chop and add	8oz/225g	Tomatoes (1 small tin)	Stir well together. Boil Lower heat. Cover pan. Cook	2 min 15 min	Hot Low
7. Slice finely	1 small	Orange	Add to the tomatoes Bring to the boil		Hot
8. Season with	 1 teasp ½ teasp 1 teasp	Salt, Pepper Garlic Tabasco Sugar	Mix well together. Cover pan and cook	15 min	Low
9. Meanwhile, grate the rind of	1 medium	Lemon	Squeeze the juice into a small bowl. Add rind		
10. Add and stir well in	2 teasp	Cornflour	Add and stir well ¼pt of the chicken water		
11. Pour into a saucepan	1 tabls	Vinegar	Add cornflour mixture		
12. Stir well in	1 teasp	Sugar	Bring to the boil and stir constantly for Lower heat. Cover pan	3 min	Med V.Low
13. Remove chicken from pan. Discard the skin			Carve the white meat very thinly (keep the legs for the next day to devil [76])		
14. Put chicken slices on a serving dish			Arrange the two sauces on either side		
15. Garnish with		Watercress	Serve		

Devilled Chicken Legs

Although legs are best, you can also use leftover cooked pieces. Serve this with an vegetable, and potatoes in their jackets, and a green salad.

Overall time:
30 min

Process	Amount	Ingredients	Explanation	Time	Heat
1. Melt	1oz/28g	Butter	In a frying pan	½ min	Hot
2. Add and fry	2	Chicken Legs	On each side for about or till tender and brown	10 min	Med
3. Add	4 tabls	Water	Stir well with a wooden spoon and scrape the sediment from the base of the pan	1 min	Hot
4. Stir well in	1 tabls	Tomato Ketchup		1 min	Med
5. Stir well in	4 teasp	Lea and Perrins			
6. Turn the legs over and over in the mixture			Coating them well	2 min	Low
7. Put chicken on a serving dish					
8. Chop finely	2 teasp	Parsley	Sprinkle over and serve		

Chicken Thighs Stuffed with Smoked Salmon Scraps in Dill Sauce

Overall time:
50 min

This is easy and quick, yet it tastes extra-special. You can buy smoked salmon scraps cheaply from any delicatessen.

Process	Amount	Ingredients	Explanation	Time	Heat
1. Chop very small	2oz/56g	Smoked Salmon Scraps	Divide into 2 little heaps. Preheat oven		Hot
2. Melt	½oz/14g	Butter	In a frying pan	½ min	Hot
3. Add and fry	4 small	Chicken Thighs (or 2 Breasts)	Till golden brown. Cook each side for about	3 min	Med
4. Transfer chicken to an ovenproof dish			Put pan with the fat aside		
5. Make a deep cut in the fleshiet part of each piece			Divide one heap of salmon between the chicken pieces. Press it into the cuts		
6. Sprinkle with		Salt Lemon Pepper	Put in oven and cook	30 min	Hot
7. After 15 mins, put	1 tabls	Cornflour	Into a bowl		
8. Add and stir well	¾pt/420ml	Milk	Pour into frying pan		
9. Return pan to heat			Boil, stirring constantly with a wooden spoon and scraping sediment from the base of the pan, for	2 min	Hot
10. Add and stir well	3 teasp	Dill Weed (fresh or dried)	Add the rest of the smoked salmon		
11. Season with	½ teasp ¼ teap	Lemon Pepper Salt	Take chicken from ovenproof dish. Pour dill sauce into dish. Mix with juices in dish and replace chicken on top		
12. Then replace dish in oven			Cook	5 min	Hot

Duck Cooked with Ginger and Orange

The pouring off of excess fat is very important for the success of this dish, which should be served with oranges peeled and sliced thinly, roast potatoes, petits pois or broccoli or sprouts and a watercress salad.

Process	Amount	Ingredients	Explanation	Time	Heat
1. Preheat the oven					Hot
2. Prick all over with a fork	2 pieces or 1 small	Duck Duckling cut in two	Sprinkle with salt		
3. Rub duck with	2 tabls	Soya Sauce	All over		
4. Rub duck with	2 teasp	Root Ginger (fresh chopped or powdered)	Over the undersides		
5. Put on a baking tray skin side up					
6. Sprinkle with		Lemon Pepper	Cook at top of oven	20 min	Hot
7. Remove from oven			Pour off the fat. Prick skin again. Return to the oven and cook	30 min	Med
8. Transfer the duck to an ovenproof dish			Return to oven	10 min	Hot
9. Pour off the fat			From the baking tray		
10. Add to tray and stir	4 tabls	Water	Boil on top of stove	1 min	Hot
11. Season with	¼ teasp	Salt Lemon Pepper	Stirring with a wooden spoon and scraping in all the sediment	1 min	Hot
12. Strain into a pan					
13. Put in a small bowl	2 teasp	Cornflour			
14. Add and mix well	6 tabls	Orange Juice (tinned or fresh)	Add this mixture to mixture in pan. Boil and stir	2 min	Hot
15. Pour this sauce all round the duck. Put		Watercress	Around it and serve		

Pheasant Stuffed and Roasted with Gravy

This is my mother's way of cooking pheasant. (A small chicken cooked exactly the same way is excellent.) Serve the pheasant with brussels sprouts, game chips or potatoes roasted in the oven with the bird, and a watercress salad.

Overall time:
¼ hr

Process	Amount	Ingredients	Explanation	Time	Heat
1. Peel and chop finely	1 medium	Onion	Preheat oven		Med
2. Melt in a saucepan	1oz/28g	Butter	Using a wooden spoon	1 min	Hot
3. Add the onions and		Salt, Pepper	Cook and stir for	5 min	Med
4. Remove crusts from	3 slices	White Bread	Crumble into a bowl add onions and butter		
5. Grate on top	1oz/28g	Cheese	Mix all well together		
6. Untruss	1	Pheasant	Stuff it with the breadcrumb mixture		
7. Rub it all over with		Salt	Put it on a baking tray		
8. Over the breast, put	3 slices	Bacon	Put it in the oven	1 hr	Med
9. Transfer pheasant to a serving dish			Keep warm in the oven		Low
10. Pour away fat in baking tray Add	¼pt/140ml	Water	Bring to the boil in the baking tray on top of the stove stirring and scraping up the sediment with a wooden spoon	1 min	Hot
11. Put in a small pan	2 teasp	Bisto			
12. Add and stir well in	3 tabls	Cold Water	Strain in the mixture from the baking tray and boil, stirring constantly for	2 min	Hot
13. Put in a gravy boat			Serve with the pheasant		

Turkey Pieces filled with Spinach Puree with a Gratinée Sauce

Overall time:
1 hr

This dish is quite rich, so serve it with plain boiled potatoes or triangles of crustless toast, and lightly boiled courgettes, peas or beans.

Process	Amount	Ingredients	Explanation	Time	Heat
1. Put in a saucepan	3 tabls	Water	Preheat oven		Med
2. Wash well and add	2oz/56g	Spinach (fresh or frozen)	Bring to the boil. Cook	4 min	Med
3. Drain and chop fine			Return to saucepan		
4. Put into a cup	4 tabls	Milk			
5. Add and mix well	2 teasp	Cornflour	Pour this over spinach		
6. Season with	¼ teasp	Nutmeg Salt, Pepper	Cook, stirring constantly Turn off heat. Cover pan	2 min	Hot
7. Melt	1oz/28g	Butter	In a frying pan	½ min	Hot
8. Add	2 each about 7oz/156g	Turkey Pieces	Fry on each side for about till golden brown	5 min	Med
9. Transfer turkey to an ovenproof dish. Sprinkle with		Salt, Pepper	Keep butter in frying pan		
10. Slit each piece horizontally with a sharp knife			Each piece should be like a pocket		
11. Sprinkle a little		Garlic Powder	Into each pocket		
12. Put into pockets	2 teasp	Butter	(1 teasp for each pocket)		
13. Divide the spinach			Between the 2 pieces of turkey, filling the pockets with spinach. Put in oven	5 min	Med
14. Add and stir well	3 teasp	Flour	Into frying pan turkey was cooked in.		
15. Add and stir well	½pt/280ml	Milk	Boil, stirring constantly with a wooden spoon, scraping the sediment from base of pan. Lower heat	2 min	Hot V.Lo
16. Grate into this	2oz/56g	Gruyère (or any cheese)	Mix well in. Pour this over turkey. Put in oven till golden brown	15 min	Hot

81 Spring Onion Crisps

Overall time: 10 mins

These are tasty served with meat or fish, or as a starter sprinkled with soya sauce.

Process	Amount	Ingredients	Explanation	Time	Heat
1. Clean and chop	10	Spring Onions	Including the green		
2. Break into a bowl	1	Egg	Beat with an eggbeater for	1 min	
3. Mix well in	3 tabls	Cornflour	Until the mixture is smooth		
4. Stir in		Salt, Pepper	Add the onions. Mix well		
5. Chop small and add	1oz/28g	Ham (optional)	Stir well together		
6. Heat in a frying pan	2 tabls	Oil	Put individual teaspoonful of the mixture into the pan to fry on each side till golden and crisp	1 min 5 min	Hot Med
7. Keep warm in oven till ready to serve					

82 Red and Yellow Peppers

Overall time: 1 hr

Particularly good with fish.

Process	Amount	Ingredients	Explanation	Time	Heat
1. Cut out the stalks of	1 and 1	Red Pepper Yellow Pepper	Remove the seeds		
2. Put the peppers on a baking tray			Cook in the oven	45 min	Med
3. Remove peppers from oven			Peel carefully, cut in strips and put in a serving dish		
4. Sprinkle over	2 tabls	Oil			
5. Season with		Salt, Pepper			
6. Chop finely	2 teasp	Parsley	Sprinkle over and serve		

83 Glazed Carrots

Well worth the little extra bit of trouble.

Overall time:
20 mins

Process	Amount	Ingredients	Explanation	Time	Heat
1. Scrape	½lb/225g	Carrots	Cut them in even lengths of about 2in/5cm, then cut them in strips about 1cm (less than ½in) wide		
2. Put in a saucepan	¼pt/140ml	Water	Add the carrots		
3. Stir in	¼ teasp	Salt	Bring to the boil	2 min	Hot
4. Add	2 teasp	Butter			
5. Stir in	1 teasp	Sugar	Cook, uncovered	10 min	Low
6. Add another	1 teasp 4 tabls	Butter Petits Pois (optional)	Cook till water has all evaporated		
7. Chop finely	1 teasp	Parsley	Sprinkle over		
8. Grind or sprinkle		Pepper	Over the carrots. Serve		

84 Carrot and Parsnip Puree

Overall time:
30 min

Process	Amount	Ingredients	Explanation	Time	Heat
1. Scrape and slice	2 medium	Carrots	Put in a saucepan		
2. Peel, slice and add	1	Parsnip	Cover with water		Hot
3. Add	½ teasp	Salt	Cover pan and cook	20 min	Med
4. Drain in a strainer			Mash with a potato masher		
5. Add and beat in	½oz/14g	Butter			
6. Season with		Salt, Pepper			
7. Chop finely	2 teasp	Parsley	Sprinkle over and serve		

Courgettes in Béchamel with Ham

An excellent accompaniment for any plain grilled meat or chicken, or with the stuffed chicken breasts with whisky, or the devilled chicken legs.

Overall time:
15 min

Process	Amount	Ingredients	Explanation	Time	Heat
1. Wash and trim	2 medium	Courgettes	Cut in slices of about ¼"/1cm thick		
2. Put in saucepan	½pt/280ml	Water	Bring to the boil	2 min	Hot
3. Add courgettes and	½ teasp	Salt	Cover pan and cook	10 min	Low
4. Meanwhile, melt	1oz/28g	Butter	In another saucepan	½ min	Hot
5. Take off heat. Stir in	2 teasp	Flour	With a wooden spoon		
6. Add and stir well	¼pt/140ml	Milk	Beat with an eggbeater	2 min	Hot
7. Stir in		Salt, Pepper			
8. Chop in bite-size bits	2oz/56g	Ham	Add to sauce. Stir well		
9. Stir well in	½ teasp	Nutmeg	Cover pan. Leave on heat		V.Low
10. Strain Courgettes			Put under cold tap for	5 secs	
11. Add courgettes to sauce			Cook and stir	1 min	Hot

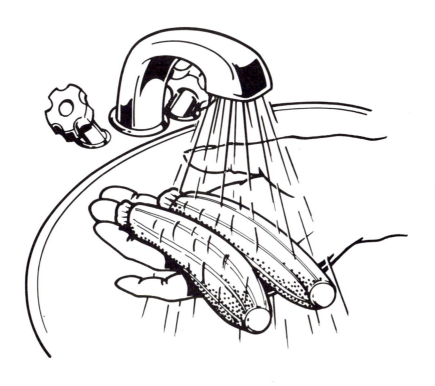

Green Beans with Celery Sticks and Spring Onions

Overall time:
25 min

Process	Amount	Ingredients	Explanation	Time	Heat
1. Cut the ends off	½lb/225g	Green French Beans	Cut beans in half if they are very long		
2. De-string	2 sticks	Celery	Cut them in lengths and then in strips, the same size as the beans		
3. Wash and trim	6	Spring Onions	Cut them the same size as the beans and celery including their long green leaves		
4. Put in a saucepan	½pt/280ml	Water	Bring to the boil	2 min	Hot
5. Add the vegetables and	½ teasp	Salt	Bring to the boil	10 min	Med
6. Strain vegetables. Put	½oz/14g	Butter	In a saucepan and melt	½ min	Hot
7. Add vegetables and		Pepper	Toss them in the butter	½ min	
8. Chop	1 teasp	Parsley	Sprinkle over and serve		

Lentils with Onions and Carrots

A very useful recipe. By adding another ¼pt water and boiling till it evaporates yo[u] have a lentil puree. By adding vinaigrette you have a lentil salad. By adding anothe[r] chicken cube and a pint of water you have a soup. As it is, it is delicious as [a] vegetable with ham or tongue or game.

Overall time:
45 mins

Process	Amount	Ingredients	Explanation	Time	Heat
1. Wash and clean well	4oz/112g	Green Lentils			
2. Bring to the boil	½pt/280ml	Water	Add lentils and stir	5 min	Hot
3. Add and stir well	½	Chicken cube	Until dissolved Lower heat		Low
4. Peel and chop very fine	½ large	Onion	Add to lentils. Stir in		
5. Scrape and grate in with the coarse side of the grater	1 large	Carrot	Stir well together. Cover pan and cook, stirring occasionally	30 min	V.Lo[w]
6. Season with		Salt, Pepper			

Broccoli with Butter Sauce

The sauce enhances the flavour of the vegetable. You can also serve it with broad beans, green beans, or courgettes. With asparagus it makes a perfect starter.

**Overall time:
30 min**

Process	Amount	Ingredients	Explanation	Time	Heat
1. Wash and trim	½lb/225g	Broccoli			
2. Put in a saucepan	½pt/280ml	Water	Bring to the boil	2 min	Hot
3. Add the broccoli and	½ teasp	Salt	Cover pan and cook	15 min	Med
4. Melt in a small pan	2oz/56g	Butter	Using a wooden spoon	1 min	Hot
5. Add and stir well	1 tabls	Flour	Take pan off heat		
6. Add gradually and stir well	¼pt/140ml	Milk	Bring to the boil Beat with an eggbeater	1 min 2 min	Hot Med
7. Stir in	½ teasp	Salt, Pepper Tarragon (optional)	Cover pan. Take off heat		
8. Strain broccoli			Put in a serving dish		
9. Pour sauce over. Chop	1 teasp	Parsley	Sprinkle over and serve		

Fried Potatoes and Onions in a Cake

A version of the famous Swiss Rosti, this is very good with roast or fried meat, or with sausages or bacon and eggs.

Overall time:
1 hr

Process	Amount	Ingredients	Explanation	Time	Heat
1. Peel and cut in 4	2 large	Potatoes	Put in a saucepan		
2. Cover with	1pt/560ml	Cold Water	Bring to the boil	4 min	Hot
3. Add	1 teasp	Salt	Lower heat and cook for	10 min	Med
4. Meanwhile, chop finely Melt in a saucepan	1 large ½oz/14g	Onion Butter	Add onions. Stir and fry	5 min	Med
5. Strain the potatoes			Put under cold tap for	1 min	
6. Grate the potatoes			Coarsely onto the onions		
7. Season with		Salt, Pepper	Mix well together		
8. Melt in a frying pan	1oz/28g	Butter		1 min	Hot
9. Add	1 tabls	Oil	Put in the potato and onion mixture and press it flat on the bottom of the pan with a fish slice		Hot
10. Cook undisturbed				15 min	Med
11. Put a plate on top			Turn frying pan upside-down so the potato cake is brown-side up on the plate		
12. Heat in pan	1 tabls	Oil	Slide potatoes off the plate into the pan. Cook	15 min	Med
13. Chop finely	2 teasp	Parsley	Sprinkle over and serve		

Potatoes Anna

Overall time:
2 hr

Process	Amount	Ingredients	Explanation	Time	Heat
1. Rub evenly	½oz/14g	Butter	Inside an ovenproof dish		
2. Peel and slice	1lb/450g	Potatoes	As finely as possible into a bowl of cold water. Leave to soak for	10 min	
3. Drain and dry them			Put a layer of potatoes in the prepared dish		
4. Cut in little pieces	3 tabls	Butter	Dot 1 tabls over potatoes		
5. Sprinkle over		Salt, Pepper	Make layers of potatoes and butter, salt and pepper		
6. Spread the top with	½oz/14g	Butter	Cover with foil and cook in the oven	45 min	Med
7. Turn dish upside-down on an ovenproof dish			Remove the cover. Return to oven for	45 min	Med
8. Pour off excess butter			Serve as a crusty cake		

Braised Endives

Overall time:
1¼ hr

With crispy bacon bits sprinkled over and crispy french bread to go with it, this is good enough for a starter, but it's perfect with any meat or chicken.

Process	Amount	Ingredients	Explanation	Time	Heat
1. Trim and wash	4 small or	Endives	Lay them in an ovenproof dish		
trim, wash and halve	2 large	Endives			
2. Sprinkle over	1 teasp	Sugar			
3. Cut over the top	1oz/28g	Butter	Cover dish with foil		
4. Put in the oven			Cook for	1hr	Med
5. Sprinkle on		Salt, Pepper			
6. Sprinkle on	1 teasp	Lemon Juice			
7. Chop finely	2 teasp	Parsley	Sprinkle on and serve		

92   Braised Leeks

Overall time:
20 min

Process	Amount	Ingredients	Explanation	Time	Heat
1. Cut in halves	4 medium	Leeks			
2. Melt in a saucepan Add	1oz/28g 4 tabls	Butter Water	Add the leeks. Turn well in the butter		Med
3. Sprinkle on		Salt, Pepper	Cover pan. Lower heat		
4. Shake the pan occasionally			Make sure the leeks are not sticking to the pan. Cook until tender	Approx 10 min	Low
5. Sprinkle on	1 teasp	Lemon Juice			
6. Chop finely	1 teasp	Parsley	Sprinkle on and serve		

93   Spinach Puree in a Sauce Béchamel

A tasty vegetable with any grilled meat, chicken or fish. It is also delicious with
poached eggs, when it becomes the famous dish called Eggs Florentine (a good
starter or light lunch dish).

Overall time:
15 min

Process	Amount	Ingredients	Explanation	Time	Heat
1. Boil	½lb/225g	Spinach (fresh or frozen)	In a saucepan with 2 tabls of water, covered for	4 min	Hot
2. Pour into a strainer			Squeeze the water out Chop very fine		
3. Melt in a small pan	1oz/28g	Butter	Using a wooden spoon	½ min	Hot
4. Stir well in	1 tabls	Flour	Take pan off heat		
5. Stir well in	¼pt/140ml	Milk	Return pan to heat and beat with an eggbeater	2 min	Hot
6. Stir in		Salt, Pepper	Add the chopped spinach. Mix well together. Lower heat. Cover pan and cook	3 min	V.Low

Basic White Sauce or Béchamel

This recipe is one of the most important of all, because it is the basis of literally hundreds of sauces and dishes. You add your flavouring at stage 5 along with the seasoning (e.g. cheese, tomato, anchovy, etc.).

**Overall time:
8 min**

Process	Amount	Ingredients	Explanation	Time	Heat
1. Melt	1oz/28g	Butter	In a saucepan	1 min	Hot
2. Add and stir well	1 tabls	Flour	Remove pan from heat		
3. Add and stir well	¼pt/140ml	Milk	Return to heat and boil, stirring constantly with a wooden spoon for	2 min	Hot
4. Lower heat			Beat with an eggbeater	2 min	Low
5. Add and stir (Add and stir	Flavour	Salt, Pepper Required)	Cook and stir for	1 min	Med
			Use at once or cover pan and leave until needed. Reheat on a medium heat beating with an eggbeater		
For a thinner sauce Add	2/3 tabls	Milk	Beat well in		
For a thicker sauce Soften	1 teasp	Butter			
Mix well with	1 teasp	Flour	Add to the sauce. Bring back to the boil and cook, stirring constantly	2 min	Med

Simple Butter Sauce

This is so good with broccoli, asparagus, cauliflower, courgettes or broad beans that you can serve them as starters; but it is also wonderful with fish, chicken or veal served with new or boiled potatoes and green beans or petits pois and carrots.

Process	Amount	Ingredients	Explanation	Time	Heat
1. Melt in a small pan	2oz/56g	Butter	Using a wooden spoon	1 min	Hot
2. Add and stir well in	2 teasp	Flour	Remove pan from heat		
3. Add and stir well in	¼pt/140ml	Milk	Beat with an eggbeater	2 min	Low
4. Season with		Salt, Pepper	Stir well together	½ min	Low
5. Add and stir well	½ teasp	Vinegar		½ min	Low
6. Add and stir well	½ teasp	Tarragon (optional)			

For a thinner sauce, delicious with simple poached fish or chicken

Add and stir well	2 tabls	White Wine	Stir with wooden spoon	1 min	Med

Hollandaise Sauce

This is a famous and delicious sauce that can be served with all manner of things . . . fish, eggs, meat, chicken or vegetables. Use a wooden spoon to beat it with – or an eggbeater, which gives it a lighter, frothy texture.

Process	Amount	Ingredients	Explanation	Time	Heat
1. Separate (see p.xv)	3	Eggs	Put yolks in a bowl (Reserve whites for something else. They will keep for 4 or 5 days in the refrigerator)		
2. Bring to the boil	3 tabls	Water	Add to yolks. Beat well		
3. Bring to the boil	½pt/280ml	Water	In a very small pan		Hot
4. Put the bowl on top			*Do not let* the bowl touch the hot water		V.Low
5. Gradually add and beat	3 teasp	Vinegar or White Wine	Continue beating over pan till it starts to thicken for about	8 min	Low
6. Cut in lumps	4oz/112g	Butter	Add this, bit by bit, beating all the time over the hot water		Low
7. Remove from heat. Add	¼ teasp	Salt	Beat well in		
8. Stir well in	½ teasp	Lemon Juice	The sauce is then ready. If you want to keep it warm for a while, cover the bowl and stand it in warm, but not hot, water		

Basic Tomato Sauce

This is one of the most useful of recipes. You can use it as a spaghetti or meat-ball sauce, as an omelette filling, with fish or shellfish and rice, with hamburgers or chicken, or vegetables. If you want a more elegant sauce you should sieve or liquidize it.

Overall time:
40 min

Process	Amount	Ingredients	Explanation	Time	Heat
1. Peel and chop finely	1 large	Onion			
2. Melt in a saucepan	2oz/56g	Butter	Using a wooden spoon	1 min	Hot
3. Add the onions			Cook, stirring constantly	5 min	Med
4. Chop small and add	1lb/450g	Tomatoes (1 medium tin)	Stir well together		
5. Season with	2 teasp	Salt, Pepper Sugar			
6. Add (chopped or dried)	2 teasp	Basil or Marjoram or Mixed Herbs			
	1	Bay Leaf	Stir well together		
7. Add and stir well	A dash	Tabasco (optional)	Cover pan. Cook for	30 min	Low

Butterscotch Sauce and Chocolate Sauce

Two useful sauces to enhance lots of sweets. You can mix them with whipped cream and serve them on their own or as a cake filling, or serve them hot or cold with ice cream.

**Overall time:
20 min**

Butterscotch Sauce

Process	Amount	Ingredients	Explanation	Time	Heat
1. Melt	1oz/28g	Butter	In a small saucepan	½ min	Hot
2. Add and stir well	2 tabls	Brown Sugar	With a wooden spoon	1 min	Med
3. Add and stir well	2 tabls	Water	Cook, stirring occasionally	10 min	Med
4. Add and stir well	2 tabls	Golden Syrup	Stir well together for	2 min	Med
5. Add	¼ teasp	Salt	Stir and cook	2 min	Low
6. Flavour with	¼ teasp	Vanilla	Serve hot or cold		

**Overall time:
10 min**

Chocolate Sauce

Process	Amount	Ingredients	Explanation	Time	Heat
1. Break in little pieces	2oz/56g	Plain Dark Chocolate	Into a small saucepan		
2. Add	1 tabls	Water	Melt, stirring constantly	3 min	Low
3. Add and stir well	1 tabls	Caster Sugar	With a wooden spoon		
4. Add and stir	½oz/14g	Butter	Mix well together	1 min	Low
5. Flavour with	1 tabls	Brandy or other liqueur (optional) or			
	1 tabls	Water	Mix well in and serve		

99 Creamed Bananas and Sherry

Serve this with little crisp biscuits or brandy snaps.

Overall time:
10 mins

Process	Amount	Ingredients	Explanation	Time	Heat
1. Peel	2	Ripe Bananas	Mash them with a fork		
2. Add	2 tabls/28g	Caster Sugar	Stir well together		
3. Whip till thick	¼pt/140ml	Cream (double or whipping)	Mix thoroughly with bananas and sugar		
4. Stir well in	4 tabls	Sherry	Till thoroughly mixed		
5. Put into a serving dish, or 2 small dishes					
6. Grate over the top	1oz/28g	Chocolate	Chill		

100 Bananas Baked with Rum and Served with Whipped Cream

Overall time:
30 mins

Process	Amount	Ingredients	Explanation	Time	Heat
1. Rub evenly	½oz/14g	Butter	Round inside an oven-proof dish. Preheat oven		Med
2. Cut in half lengthways	2	Ripe Bananas	Lay in the dish		
3. Sprinkle over	2 tabls	Brown Sugar			
4. Squeeze juice from	1	Lemon	Sprinkle over		
5. Sprinkle over	1 tabls	Water			
6. Sprinkle over	3 tabls	Rum			
7. Chop in small bits	½oz/14g	Butter	Sprinkle over. Put in the oven and cook	20 min	Med
8. Whip till thick	4 tabls	Cream (double or whipping)	Serve together		

Lemon and Vodka Mousse

A most refreshing pudding, with or without vodka.

Overall time:
30 mins

Process	Amount	Ingredients	Explanation	Time	Heat
1. Put in a small pan	2 tabls	Cold Water			
2. Add and stir	2 teasp	Gelatine	Dissolve gently	1 min	Med
3. Grate the rind of	1 large	Lemon	Squeeze the juice into a small bowl		
4. Add and stir well			The gelatine mixture and the rind		
5. Add and stir well	1 tabls	Vodka (optional)	Put in the refrigerator	20 min	
6. Separate (see p.xv)	1 large	Egg	Into two small bowls		
7. Add to the yolk	2 tabls	Sugar	Beat with an eggbeater	2 min	
8. Add the lemon mixture			Beat well together	2 min	
9. Wash the eggbeater and *dry well*			Beat the white till it forms stiff peaks	Approx 1 min	
10. Combine ingredients			Fold them carefully together (see p.xv). Put in a serving dish or in two glass dishes and chill till set		

Negresse en Chemise

Overall time:
2 hrs

Process	Amount	Ingredients	Explanation	Time	Heat
1. Heat in a saucepan	¼pt/140ml	Milk		1 min	Hot
2. Break up and add	4oz/112g	Plain Dark Chocolate	Melt in the milk		Low
3. Crush into crumbs	12	Sponge Fingers	Add to saucepan. Mix well. Remove from heat		
4. Put in a mixing bowl	2oz/56g	Butter			
5. Add and beat well	2oz/56g	Sugar	With an electric whisk or a wooden spoon for or till creamy light	5–8 min	
6. Separate (see p.xv)	2	Eggs	Put whites in a bowl and beat yolks into the butter and sugar		
7. Add the chocolate sponge mixture to yolk mixture			Beat well		
8. Whip the eggwhites			With an eggbeater for till stiff peaks form	2 min	
9. Fold eggwhites into chocolate mixture			(see p.xv)		
10. Rub evenly	1 teasp	Butter	Inside a ring mould or an ovenproof bowl. Pour in the mixture		
11. Place this in a baking tin ¼ full of		Hot Water	Cook in the oven	45 min	Med
12. Turn out onto a dish					
13. Put in a small bowl Add and stir	3 tabls 3 or 4 teasp	Icing Sugar Water	Spread over the top of the chocolate mould		
14. Whip until thick	¼pt/140ml	Cream (double or whipping)	Serve with pudding, hot or cold		

Sweet Cream Cheese Flan with Lemon, Nuts and Raisins

Overall time:
¼ hr

Process	Amount	Ingredients	Explanation	Time	Heat
1. Roll into crumbs	8 Sweet	Wholemeal Biscuits	With a rolling pin		
2. Melt in a saucepan	2oz/56g	Butter	Add crumbs. Mix well	3 min	Hot
3. Put this mixture into a 7"/18cm flan dish (or cake tin)			Press it firmly over the base, into the corners and up the sides		
4. Separate (see p.xv)	2	Eggs	Into two different bowls		
5. Add to the yolks	4 tabls	Sugar	Beat with an eggbeater	3 min	
6. Add and beat in	8oz/225g	Cream Cheese	Preheat oven		Med
7. Grate in the rind of	1 large	Lemon	Squeeze in the juice and beat well		
8. Chop small and add	1oz/28g	Almonds			
9. Stir in	1oz/28g	Raisins			
10. Stir in	1oz/28g	Candied Peel (optional)			
11. Stir in	1 tabls	Sherry (optional)			
12. Melt and add	½oz/14g	Butter	Mix all well together		
13. Wash the eggbeater and *dry well*			Beat the eggwhites till they become stiff peaks for	2 min	
14. Fold in (see p.xv)			With the other ingredients (using metal spoon)		
15. Pour this into flan dish or tin			Cook in the oven	40 min	Med

Creamy Apricot Compôte

Soaking time:
4 hr
Cooking time:
30 min

This is delicious served with brandy snaps or fresh pineapple. I usually decorate :
with slices of fresh fruit.

Process	Amount	Ingredients	Explanation	Time	Heat
1. Put in a bowl	4oz/112g	Dried Apricots	Cover with water and soak	3-4 hr or overnight	
2. In a saucepan, put	3 tabls	Demerara Sugar	Pour the apricots and water on top. Mix well, cover pan and boil	15 min	Med
3. Remove the fruit with a perforated spoon			Bring the liquid back to the boil. Cook	5 min	Hot
4. Cut the fruit in small pieces			Put in a bowl and pour the syrup over them. Chill		
5. In a small bowl, whip	4 tabls	Cream (double or whipping)	Till thick		
6. Add and stir in	4 tabls	Yoghourt	Stir in the fruit and syrup		
7. Sprinkle over	1 teasp	Cinnamon	Stir well into the other ingredients		
8. Spoon the mixture into a serving dish			Decorate with slices of fresh fruit if you like		
9. Chop finely	2 tabls	Almonds	Sprinkle over the top and chill until needed		

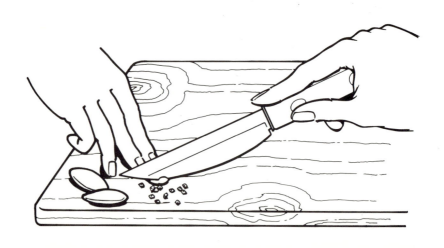

Poached Peaches with Raspberry Sauce

Serve with whipped cream or with a good vanilla ice cream.

Overall time:
1 hr

Process	Amount	Ingredients	Explanation	Time	Heat
1. Bring to the boil	1pt/560ml	Water	In a small saucepan	4 min	Hot
2. Put in	2	Peaches	Cook gently for	6 min	V.Low
3. Drain in a strainer			Peel peaches and chill		
4. Meanwhile, put	8oz/225g	Raspberries	In a saucepan		
5. Add and stir	3 tabls	Sugar	Bring to the boil for	2 min	Hot
6. Put through a sieve			To remove all the seeds		
7. Put peaches in a bowl			Serve with the raspberry sauce		

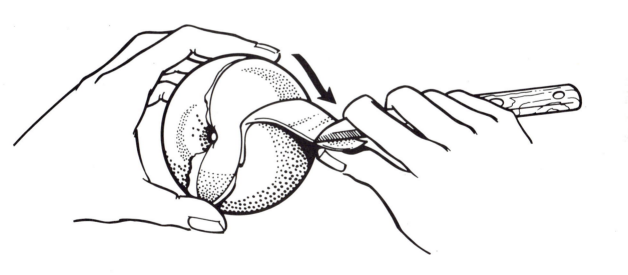

Pineapple Halves filled with Raisin, Rum and Ginger Cream

**Overall time:
1 hr**

Decorate this with a sprig of fresh mint, or slices of kiwi fruit, if you like.

Process	Amount	Ingredients	Explanation	Time	Heat
1. Put in a small pan	1 tabls	Water			
2. Add	1 tabls	Rum			
3. Add and stir	1 tabls	Raisins	Cook gently till the liquid has evaporated	5 min	Low
4. Cut in half lengthways	1 small	Pineapple	Cut the flesh out as well as you can to keep its rounded shape		
5. Discard the hard middle bits			Slice the two pieces of pineapple flesh into 6 or 7 arc-shaped slices		
6. Cool the raisins			Scrape out the skins of the pineapple with a spoon and mix the scrapings with the raisins		
7. Chop very small	½ tabls	Preserved Ginger	Mix with raisins		
8. Whip till thick	¼pt/140ml	Cream (double or whipping)			
9. Add and stir well	2 tabls	Sugar	Mix this well with the raisin mixture and fill the pineapple halves with it		
10. Put on a serving dish			Decorate with the pineapple slices and chill until needed		

Little Pots of Chocolate Marquise

Serve this with fresh or whipped cream. It will keep for days in the freezer.

Overall time:
20 mins

Process	Amount	Ingredients	Explanation	Time	Heat
1. Separate (see p.xv)	1 large	Egg	Putting the white in one small bowl and the yolk in another		
2. In a small pan, boil	½pt/280ml	Water	Lower heat and put a third bowl over pan		V.Low
3. Break into this bowl	4oz/112g	Plain Dark Chocolate	In little bits		
4. Add and stir	2oz/56g	Butter	Melt and mix well with the chocolate. Take off the heat		Low
5. Add to yolk	3 tabls	Icing Sugar	Beat with an eggbeater	2 min	
6. Combine this with the melted chocolate			Beat well together. Wash eggbeater and *dry thoroughly*		
7. Whip the eggwhite			With the eggbeater till it makes stiff peaks	1 min	
8. Fold this (see p.xv)			Into the other ingredients very carefully with a big metal spoon		
9. Pour into little pots or ramekin dishes			Chill till needed		

French Apple Tart

This can be served hot, but don't burn yourself when you turn it upside down! It is the famous Tarte Tatin.

Overall time:
1 hr

Process	Amount	Ingredients	Explanation	Time	Heat
1. Put in a small pan	4 tabls	Brown Sugar	Preheat oven		Med
2. Add and stir well	1 tabls	Water	Cook and stir with a wooden spoon till sugar is completely melted	5 min	Med
3. Pour into a cake tin or flan dish			Tilt the dish till the base is completely covered		
4. Peel, core and slice Sprinkle over these	5 eating ½ a ¼ teasp	Apples Lemon's Juice Cinnamon	Very thinly. Put them overlapping, all around the sugared dish		
5. Put in a bowl	4 tabls	Flour			
6. Cut in tiny bits	1oz/28g	Butter	Over the flour		
7. Mix in	1 tabls	Sugar	Mix these well together using your fingertips and rubbing the butter into the flour till it is like breadcrumbs		
8. Mix well in	2 teasp	Water	Spread this pastry over the apples as evenly as you can		
9. Press down very well			Put in the oven. Cook	40 min	Med
10. Remove from oven			Leave to cool. Put a plate on top of the dish or tin and turn it upside down		
11. Remove the tin			Serve when needed		

Light Iced Sponge with Raspberry, Sherry Cream Filling and Whipped Cream

Overall time:
½ hr

This is equally good with strawberries. Have a few extra fruits to decorate the surrounding cream. It makes a delicious birthday cake and you can make a big one as easily using double quantities and 10 min extra in the oven.

Process	Amount	Ingredients	Explanation	Time	Heat
1. Rub evenly	¼oz/7g	Butter	Round insides of 2 cake tins (size 7″/18cm) Preheat oven		Med
2. Shake	1 teasp	Flour	All round insides of tins		
3. Break into a bowl	3	Eggs	Beat with an eggbeater	2 min	
4. Add and beat in	6 tabls	Sugar	With eggbeater (or mixer)	5 min	
5. Sieve on top of eggs	6 tabls	Self-raising Flour	Using a big metal spoon, fold (see p.xv) together		
6. Pour into cake tins			Allowing half the mixture to each tin. Put in oven	20 min	Med
7. Remove from oven			Run a knife around between the sides of the cakes and the tins		
8. Turn cakes out onto a wire tray			Allow to cool		
9. Put in a bowl	8oz/225g	Raspberries or Strawberries	Mash well with a fork		
10. Pour over	2 tabls	Sherry			
11. Sprinkle over	3 tabls	Sugar	Mix well together		
12. Whip until thick	½pt/280ml	Cream (double or whipping)	Combine all together		
13. Split cakes in half horizontally			Spread cream mixture evenly over tops of three of the halves. Sandwich all four halves together		
14. Put in a small bowl	9 tabls	Icing Sugar			
15. Add and stir well	3 teasp	Hot Water	When smooth, spread evenly over cake with a knife dipped in very hot water		
16. Whip until thick	¼pt/140ml	Cream (as above)	Spread around the sides of the cake with a fork		

Iced Chocolate Sponge Cake with Rich Chocolate Filling and Whipped Cream

This cake is perfect for a birthday surprise or special occasion. (It takes no longer i the preparation to make a big one but 10 mins more in the oven.)

Process	Amount	Ingredients	Explanation	Time	Heat
1. Rub evenly	¼oz/7g	Butter	Over insides of 2 cake tins (size 7"/18cm) Preheat oven		Med
2. Shake	1 teasp	Flour	Round insides of tins		
3. Break into a bowl	3	Eggs	Beat with an eggbeater	2 min	
4. Beat in	6 tabls	Sugar	With eggbeater (or mixer)	5 min	
5. Sieve on top of eggs	4 tabls	Self-raising Flour			
6. Then sieve on top	2 tabls	Cocoa	Fold (see p.xv) all together		
7. Pour into cake tins			Allowing half the mixture to each tin. Put in oven	20 min	Med
8. Remove from oven			Run a knife around between the sides of the cakes and the tins		
9. Turn cakes out			Onto a wire tray to cool		
10. Put	4oz/56g	Butter	In a mixing bowl		
11. Add and beat well	8 tabls	Icing Sugar	With mixer or wooden spoon till it is white and light	5 min	
12. Put into a cup	2 tabls	Cocoa			
13. Add and mix well in	4 teasp	Water	Add this to butter mixture Beat thoroughly for	3 min	
14. Add and beat well	2 tabls	Liqueur (optional)	Spread this mixture all over one cake. Put the other on top		
15. Put in a small bowl	6 tabls	Icing Sugar			
16. Add	2 tabls	Cocoa			
17. Add and stir well	3 teasp	Hot Water	Until it is very smooth		
18. Pour this onto cake			Spread evenly over top, with a knife dipped in very hot water		
19. Whip till thick	¼pt/140ml	Cream (double or whipping)	Spread around the sides of the cake with a fork		
20. Sprinkle		Chocolate Vermicelli	Over the top and sides		

Index